CW01667283

BULGARIA

TRADITION & BEAUTY

Edited by
Elizabeth I. Kwasnik

NATIONAL MUSEUMS & GALLERIES
· ON MERSEYSIDE ·

The exhibition will also be seen at:
The Ulster Folk and Transport Museum 1990
Leeds City Museum 1990-91

This exhibition is organised with the
Ethnographic Institute with Museum
of the Bulgarian Academy of Sciences, Sofia.

British Library Cataloguing
in Publication Data available.

First published in Great Britain by
National Museums & Galleries on Merseyside.

ISBN 0 906367 38 7

Printed by Lund Humphries, Bradford. Typeset by P's & Q's Liverpool.

Contents

Preface

Reaching westwards into eastern Europe from the shores of the Black Sea, Bulgaria is bordered by Romania, Yugoslavia and Greece. Like many countries on the continent of Europe it has withstood substantial geo-political changes at the hands of foreign powers including occupation by the Turks for 500 years when Bulgaria was part of the Ottoman Empire. What has maintained Bulgaria's cultural indentity is its material culture: its traditional costumes; wood-carving; ceramics; metalwork; jewellery; embroidery and architecture.

The exhibition for which this booklet is written is the result of two years cooperation between Liverpool Museum, of the National Museums and Galleries on Merseyside, and the Ethnographic Institute with Museum of the Bulgarian Academy of Sciences in Sofia, Bulgaria's capital city.

Liverpool Museum cannot claim to be the first British museum to present an exhibition of Bulgarian artefacts. The exhibition 'Village Arts' in the Museum of Mankind in London in 1977 was probably the first time Bulgarian ethnographic material had been extensively displayed in Britain. The material was subsequently donated to the British Museum by the Bulgarian Committee for Culture. Unfortunately, apart from the collection in the British Museum, there are virtually no museums in Britain with any more than a few Bulgarian items and most of those are poorly documented.

However, there is an important collection in private hands belonging to Dan Lumley and Diane Waller of Brighton. It contains examples of Yugoslavian and Bulgarian costume and artefacts and is complemented by a comprehensive library of Balkan ethnographic literature.

Liverpool Museum is the first British museum to present a comprehensive exhibition of traditional Bulgarian artefacts. Some 600 items are presented in 13 thematic groups. Such is the variety of objects essential to the appreciation of Bulgarian traditional life that it would not have been possible to include a satisfactory explanation of them all within the exhibition itself.

In the chapters which make up this booklet a number of distinguished Bulgarian scholars have written about their specialist interests. Academician Veselin Hadjinikolov traces the roots of Bulgarian folk culture back to a fusion of Thracian, Slav and Proto-Bulgarian features. Commenting on traditional culture today he welcomes both its relevance and survival but he indicates that its guardians have changed from the members of an agrarian society to that of a group of professional specialists, composers, artists, architects, museum workers and the like.

Other contributors deal with the evolution of Bulgarian vernacular architecture and the influence of the National Revival on the style of traditional houses before the intervention of European notions of classicism. We learn too of the functional layout of the house, the domestic use of the brilliant textiles and intricately carved woodwork. The life, folklore and woodcarving skills of the shepherds are discussed, and the skills of the metalworker and the potter are revealed. Bulgaria is well known for the competence and artistry of its embroideries, particularly in the context of the decoration they provide for the traditional costumes, the stunning variety of which are fully discussed here.

One of the fascinations of Bulgaria is its custom and belief and the extent to which some of the traditional rituals and festivals are still observed today. We are fortunate to have a comprehensive and instructive review of the most significant of these. Finally there is an assessment of what traditional custom and practice mean to the Bulgarians today in their search for their cultural indentity.

In preparing the exhibition and in editing this booklet I have received advice and assistance from many friends and colleagues. I would however like to express my thanks in particular to Vesela Vassileva for her patience, guidance and perseverance and to Diane Waller, Dan Lumley, Dr. Venetia Newall and Michael Holman. Special thanks go also to Richard Foster, Keith Robinson, the Design staff, Helen Thornton and Lynne Stumpe for their support and encouragement.

Elizabeth I. Kwasnik.

Foreword

The idea of holding the exhibition 'Bulgaria – Tradition and Beauty' emerged after a visit to Liverpool Museum by the then Bulgarian Ambassador His Excellency Mr. Kiril Shterev. At that time the British Museum was displaying the newly-discovered Thracian treasure from Rogozen. The success of this exhibition prompted the thought that an exhibition which looked at the more recent history of the Bulgarian people might reflect the growing interest in this part of Eastern Europe now undergoing fundamental social and economic change. The keen interest of Mr. Zhulev, who succeeded Mr. Shterev in 1987 and of Professor Roumen Katincharov ensured the support of the Bulgarian government and the Bulgarian academic community.

At the invitation of the Bulgarian Committee of Culture discussions took place in 1987 and 1988 between the respective staffs of the Ethnographical Institute with Museum, Sofia and the Department of Archaeology and Ethnology of Liverpool Museum. The content of an exhibition was evolved that would draw the attention of both specialists and the general public to the rich and varied material culture, custom and belief of the Bulgarian people, throwing light particularly on the achievements of the Bulgarian National Revival in the late eighteenth and early nineteenth centuries.

The exhibition, of which this booklet is an integral part, reveals a nation rich in folk tradition and material culture, much of whose rural population did not feel the impact of industrialisation until the 1950's and 1960's. A substantial programme of fieldwork, research and publication has been undertaken by the Bulgarian Academy of Sciences through scholars attached to the Ethnographic Institute with Museum in Sofia which has succeeded in recording much of the traditional way of life before it disappeared.

The mounting of the exhibition, the holding of the symposium and the preparation of this publication would not have been possible without the kind cooperation and committed involvement of Academician Hadjinikolov, Professor G. Georgiev, Dr. Ignat Minkov, Miss Vesela Vassileva and the several contributing authors to this booklet. Much assistance has also been received from Academician Angelov and Mrs Svetlana Nikolova of the Centre for Bulgarian Studies, Sofia. We are most grateful to Dr. Peter Shopov, Bulgarian Cultural Counsellor, whose energy and ability in overcoming the many administrative and technical problems has been outstanding.

We have been greatly assisted by many British scholars who gave freely of their time and advice in the early stages of the project, particularly Michael Holman and Diane Waller.

Our thanks in particular must go to Elizabeth Kwasnik, Curator of North American. Arctic and Oceanic Collections, for her skill and dedication in undertaking all the curatorial work on the exhibition, organising the symposium and for editing this publication. We would also acknowledge our debt to Keith Robinson, the Design and Production Manager, and his staff for overcoming many technical difficulties and producing the exhibition.

Finally the Trustees express their pleasure that the exhibition will travel to Ulster and Leeds following its Liverpool showing.

Richard Foster, Director,
National Museums and Galleries on Merseyside.

Acknowledgements

The Trustees of the National Museums and Galleries on Merseyside acknowledge the generous assistance of the following:

The Lyudmila Zhivkova International Foundation.

Balkan Holidays Ltd.

Bulgarian Vintners Company Ltd.

The British Council (Visiting Arts).

The University of Liverpool.

Ocean Transport and Trading plc.

The Committee for Culture, People's Republic of Bulgaria.

The Bulgarian Academy of Sciences.

The Ethnographic Institute with Museum, Sofia.

The British Embassy, Sofia.

Michael Holman.

Dan Lumley.

Diane Waller.

A Culture with Millennial Traditions and Achievements

Academician Veselin Hadjinikolov
Member of the Bulgarian Academy of Sciences

The culture of every nation is the conscious creativity of the people. It has its strata which differ first in their chronology and, secondly, in the position and social identification of the people creating and using them. There are two principal layers of culture of the second type. On the one hand the official, professional culture of the elite and on the other - folk, traditional and everyday culture.

The folk, traditional or everyday culture is created by anonymous authors who have received their knowledge and skills through tradition or through the spiritual bridge between the generations. Its aim is to satisfy the vital, aesthetic, communicative, routine and normal requirements of the ordinary people. This is a stratum with millennial traditions and achievements, which has inexhaustible wisdom and beauty concentrated within it.

This is an age of scientific and technological revolution, of intensive and convenient international communications, of creative manifestations of many talents in the sphere of the material, spiritual and cultural life. As such it emphasises and attaches importance to official and professional culture. Folk or traditional culture is usually kept in museums, in the repertoire of the folklore ensembles and in the storage chests of our mothers and grandmothers. This is probably why traditional culture evokes an ever increasing interest and justified admiration, especially among the younger generations.

Bulgarian folk culture also has its deep historical roots that can be traced far back in the millennia. Some researchers assume that it was in the present-day Bulgarian lands and in the Balkan Peninsula, a long, long time ago, that man first began to cultivate cereal crops and started to grow vines and fruit-bearing trees. Crafts, especially those of the jewellers and potters, produced remarkable works. This is revealed by the many gold and silver treasures left by the Thracians and even by their predecessors all being found in Bulgaria (e.g. the treasures from Varna, Rogozen, Panagjurishte, and Vulchitrun.) The Varna treasure, which was discovered not so long ago near the Black Sea resort of the same name, it is suggested dates from the Chalcolithic Age (5000-6000 BC).

The roots of Bulgarian folk culture can be sought in the core of the three components that have led to the emergence of the Bulgarian nation: first, the Thracians who were among the oldest inhabitants of the Balkan Peninsula; secondly, the Slavs who settled in the Balkan provinces of the Byzantine Empire in the 6th-7th century and, thirdly, the Proto-Bulgarians who came from the Volga steppes. This occurred when the Bulgarian ethnic community finally took shape as a nation in the 9th-10th century with the Slavs providing its language and basic cultural characteristics and the Proto-Bulgarians contributing their ethnic name. The Slavonic-Bulgarian language and the adoption of Christianity in the 9th century fulfilled a very important role in bringing about ethnic and cultural cohesion.

Thus, in the course of its development, Bulgarian folk culture was characterised by a peculiar cultural syncretism; (1) It was a homogeneous amalgam of Thracian, Slav and Proto-Bulgarian features, possessing an ancient colour, Slav predominance and eastern proto-Bulgarian specificity; (2) It comprised pagan characteristics combined with Christian cultural elements; (3) This original cultural amalgam with its own stylistic features was complemented by Hellenic, Byzantine, Western European and other elements.

Bulgarian folk culture, like all folk cultures, is characterised by a certain conservatism conditioned by its traditionality and mandatory stereotypes. In itself, conservatism slowed down the cultural processes, but at the same time it was one of the most important factors which saved the Bulgarian people from attempts by the Ottoman Empire to assimilate them during its domination over the Bulgarian lands from the 15th to the 19th centuries. Deprived of his state, oppressed and subjected to merciless exploitation by the Ottoman enslaver, the Bulgarian survived on the strength of his communal and church institutions, as well as those of his folk culture, which he developed further and enriched.

According to the evidence of foreign travellers in the

Ottoman Empire, the Bulgarian people and predominantly the Bulgarian woman created for themselves and for their homes magnificent woven cloths, garments, embroidery, knitting, multicoloured bed linen and towels, exquisite works of folk art, which strengthened their patriotism and their sense of dignity. From the 16th century onward and above all during the Bulgarian National Revival period (18th-19th century) various crafts practised in workshops flourished in Bulgaria. Dozens of such crafts existed and they satisfied the vital, aesthetic and religious needs of both Bulgarians and Ottomans, and their fame spread all over the Empire.

After the liberation of Bulgaria from Ottoman domination in 1878, when the country started along the road of industrial development, the unitary nature of folk culture began to disintegrate. The villages in which more than 80% of the population lived until the end of the Second World War remained its principal territory. The towns and cities were dominated by the culture of manufacture, factories and standardised production, which increasingly fell under the influence of Western modes of life and fashion. In the 1930's Western fashion penetrated deeply into the intelligentsia and the affluent elite in the villages.

The intensified industrialisation of the People's Republic of Bulgaria in the 1950's and 1960's, the collectivisation of agriculture, the country's rapid urbanisation and its housing revolution minimised the role of folk culture in everyday life. Only a small number of traditional tools and production practices remained in use: in tobacco growing and in the cultivation of other industrial crops; in high-mountainous stockbreeding; in the private farms and in the out-of -town cottages. The national cuisine, the practice of the folk healers, the work of traditional craftsmen, the original performances of folklore by ensembles, by amateur performers and by famous folk singers and instrumentalists have preserved their unique folk identity.

Bulgarian folk culture today can be said to enjoy a secondary life-style, that is, it is recreated through the intervention of professional specialists such as composers, artists, architects, museum workers and others. It is through their efforts that the older residential and artisan areas are reconstructed and ancient buildings restored. Folk songs and dances are acquiring an ever greater attraction for the modern person with a new aesthetic taste. Folk creativity is also coming alive in applied arts, in the works of the eminent composers, writers, poets and artists who are using traditional stylistic features, ornaments, colours, rhythms and tones.

The Ethnographic Institute with Museum of the Bulgarian Academy of Sciences

Ignat Minkov

The Ethnographic Institute with Museum of the Bulgarian Academy of Sciences unites two mutually complementary institutions: an academic institute and a museum with a national programme. Their fusion was a natural consequence of the lengthy development of Bulgarian ethnographic science and museum work, which started as early as the first half of the 19th century.

The interest in Bulgarian culture grew among the Bulgarians in their aspirations to establish themselves as an independent nation in the conditions of slavery within the multi-national Ottoman Empire. This interest was also stimulated by the studies of the folk traditions which were developing at that time in the European countries. Even in the 1830's, a number of outstanding figures of the Bulgarian National Revival carried out historical and ethnographic studies, publishing the first folk songs and investigations on the way of life of the people, organising the first ethnographic exhibitions and making attempts to build a historical-ethnographic museum. Under the conditions of the Ottoman Empire, however, all these activities were extremely hampered.

Irrespective of the various obstacles, the ethnographic studies of foreign and Bulgarian researchers and the social struggles of the Bulgarian people for Church and political independence from the mid-19th century onward clearly outlined the characteristics and boundaries of Bulgarian people.

After the country's liberation from Ottoman domination in 1878, the first state-financed public and cultural institutions, including the first museums, were built. The National Museum was opened in Sofia in 1892, and in 1906 it became the independent institution of the National Ethnographic Museum under the direct guidance of the Ministry of Education.

In the next four decades the museum gained prestige as the principal national centre of Bulgarian ethnographic science. Extensive collecting activities and research spread over the entire ethnic territory of the Bulgarian people. Parallel with the material finds, folkloric and auxiliary scientific materials were also collected, and a specialized ethnographic-folkloristic library was also set up.

The most outstanding Bulgarian ethnographers and folklorists work in the Museum or co-operate with it. As well as publishing numerous monographic works, the Museum also produced fourteen large volumes in its series *Bulletin of the National Ethnographic Museum* between 1926 and 1943.

In addition to the numerous and varied exhibitions and scientific events organised in the country to promote ethnography, the Ethnographic Museum enjoyed a vast international activity as well. Papers were presented at many scientific forums. Several Bulgarian ethnographic exhibitions have been held abroad: Anvers, 1894; Paris, 1900 and 1937; Saint Louis, 1904; Liege, 1905; Prague, 1912 and 1937; Berlin and Geneva, 1916; London, 1922 and 1928; New York, 1923; Warsaw, 1928; The Hague, 1930; Rome, 1931 and Helsinki, 1937.

During that period ethnographic research was in progress not only at the National Ethnographic Museum, but also at the Departments of History and Slavonic Studies at the Kliment Ohridski University of Sofia. This cooperation brought about the publishing of the *Miscellany for Folk Wisdom Science and Literature* - a fundamental edition for Bulgarian folk culture. Founded in 1889 it is published to this day by the Bulgarian Academy of Sciences with several volumes produced so far. Other scientific and specialised publications continue to be produced.

After the Second World War the people's democratic rule in Bulgaria created much better conditions for organising ethnographic research. An ethnographic institute was set up in 1947 at the Bulgarian Academy of Sciences, to which the National Ethnographic Museum was added in 1949. This led to the emergence of the Ethnographic Institute with Museum of the Bulgarian Academy of Sciences as it exists today. During that period and later, specialists from the Institute and from the Museum were instrumental in producing differentiation in the study of Bulgarian folk culture.

As Ethnographers mastered their subject matter the science itself was transformed from a purely culturological to a historical discipline providing a view of Bulgarian people and culture. The research activities of the Institute comprise historical ethnography and ethnogenesis of the Bulgarian people, the material, spiritual and social culture, livelihood and art, urban ethnography and studies of contemporary Bulgarian people. Parallel with individual research, the practice of collective research is also gaining ground resulting in the appearance of many interesting ethnographic collections of a complex nature, published in addition to the thematic and monographic editions. Scientific contacts and joint research projects have been established with similar scientific organisations both in Bulgaria and abroad.

Since 1953 the Institute has published annually its *Bulletin of the Ethnographic Institute with Museum of the Bulgarian Academy of Sciences*, transformed since 1975 into the *Bulgarian Ethnography* series with four issues per year. *Ethnography of Bulgaria* (in three volumes), published in the mid-eighties, could be viewed as a sort of generalisation of the Institute's research activities.

The National Ethnographic museum is now working under much better conditions. Fortunately, the ethnographic collections destroyed during the bombing raids over Sofia during the war are being rapidly replaced and they now comprise nearly 50,000 original objects divided into thirteen different deposits. The museum collection is extensively used for the purpose of research and education, as well as for exhibitions. The Museum is providing methodological assistance and consultations to local and regional ethnographic museums, departments and museum collections , to artists and craftsmen practising folk crafts and also to scholars and specialists.

The activities of the Museum abroad have also become richer. After the Second World War representative ethnographic exhibitions were organised in the capitals of the socialist countries, as well as in Paris, Pittsburg, Linz, Brussels, Erevan, Tokyo and among the Bulgarian ethnic population living in Australia, Argentina and elsewhere.

Having accumulated rich archives and museum collections, the specialists working at the Ethnographic Institute with Museum of the Bulgarian Academy of Sciences are currently engaged in the major project of writing a 10-volume *Ethnography of Bulgaria.* The National Ethnographic Museum also looks forward to becoming the nucleus of the National Ethnographic Park-Museum which is to be built near Sofia in the near future.

With the organising of the ethnographic exhibition BULGARIA - TRADITION & BEAUTY and owing to the kind help and enterprising spirit of the Liverpool Museum, the Ethnographic Institute with Museum of the Bulgarian Academy of Sciences expresses the willingness of the Bulgarian people to exchange their cultural values with the peoples of the United Kingdom, and to live with them in peace, friendship and cooperation.

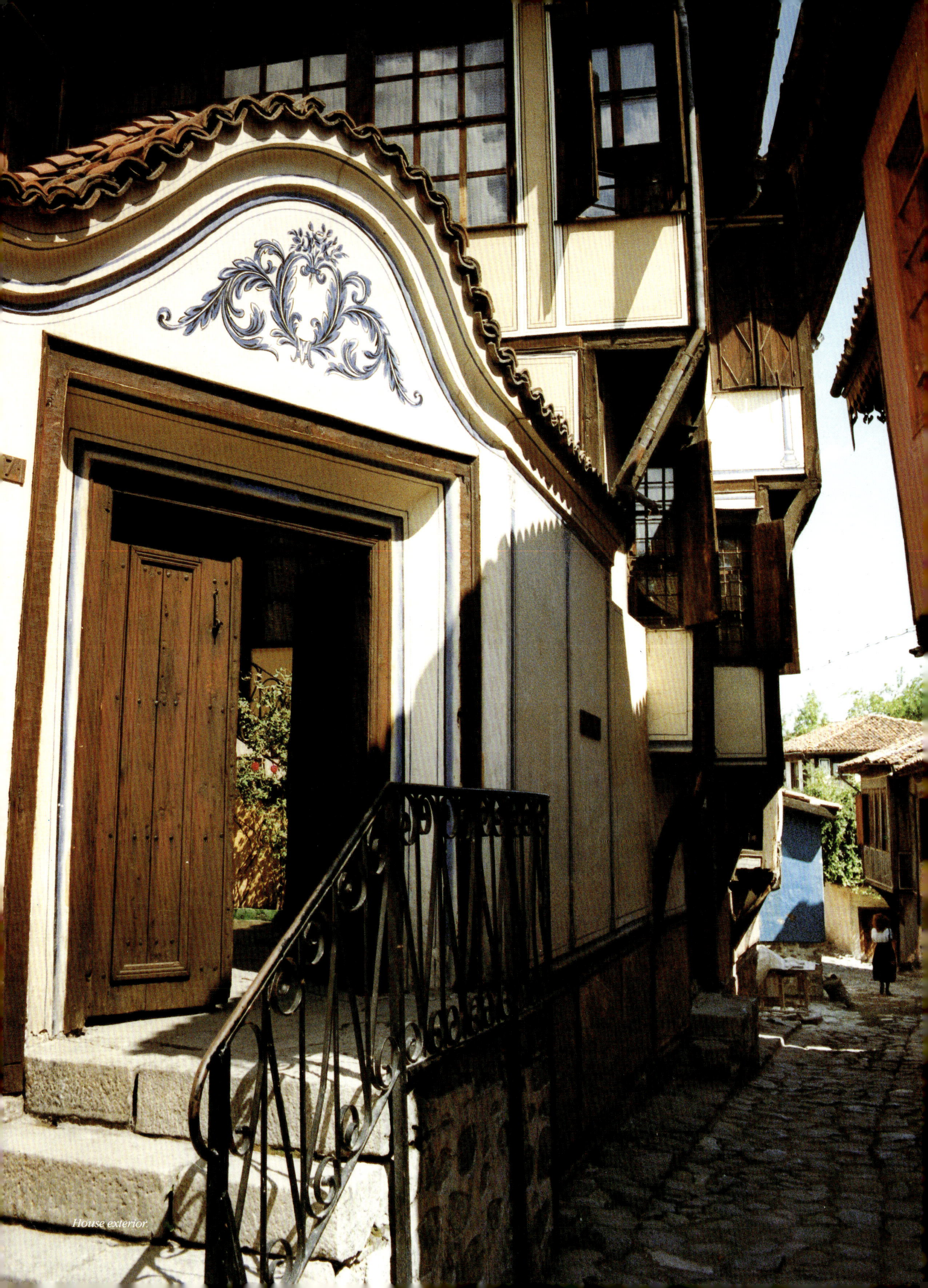

House exterior

Architecture, Organisation and Furniture

Snezhana Dimitrova

The material environment of the home has always been one of the most essential aspects of the culture of every traditional society. Being the most immediate living environment for people, it demonstrates a great variety of forms among the Bulgarians, resulting from the constant struggle for better living conditions and reflecting the influence of the most varied natural, geographic and social factors.

The building and architectural heritage of the Balkans became a meeting point for the building perceptions and technologies of Slavs and Proto-Bulgarians with the building traditions of the ancient indigenous population enriched by the positive influence of the great ancient civilisations of Greece and Rome. Later, during the Ottoman domination over the Bulgarian lands (14th-19th century), the Oriental influence began to be felt, albeit slightly.

Thus in the course of their centuries-long historical development the Bulgarians created a local original architecture and domestic environment akin to that of neighbouring Balkan nations that reflected in a most immediate manner the conditions of agricultural, stockbreeding and artisan production. The evolution of these building forms may be assessed primarily on the basis of isolated examples of some types of houses that have survived even since the second half of the 19th century. The characteristic features of the traditional types of house are also indirectly detected in the forms of the more highly developed architecture of the Bulgarian National Revival period in the 18th and 19th centuries both in the villages and urban centres. In this sense the typical house of the National Revival period can be regarded as a distinct peak in the development of the traditional Bulgarian house, a peak attained before it became influenced by European architecture.

Traditional Bulgarian architecture also includes buildings associated with activities of other than local significance such as fortresses, fortified administrative and residential buildings, tower- houses, farm buildings, as well as bridges, fountains, bazaars, cultural buildings (churches, monasteries and even mosques) erected by the Bulgarians in the spirit of Bulgarian building traditions.

The traditional Bulgarian house demonstrates a remarkable wealth of forms, shapes and variants. The houses that have survived reveal rigorous specificity from the point of view of planning, the number of storeys, the building structures and the materials used. The great variety in the Bulgarian landscape and the mountainous nature of the terrain have evoked numerous variations in the housing styles. These are reflected locally in the layout of the courtyard and its relationship with the other houses and farm buildings. Together they produce the plan and the general appearance of the town or village.

In a historical plan the dwelling evolved from a single-room home with a fireplace, to the multipartite house as a result of adding new rooms or by dividing the already existing ones. In this way the most common,

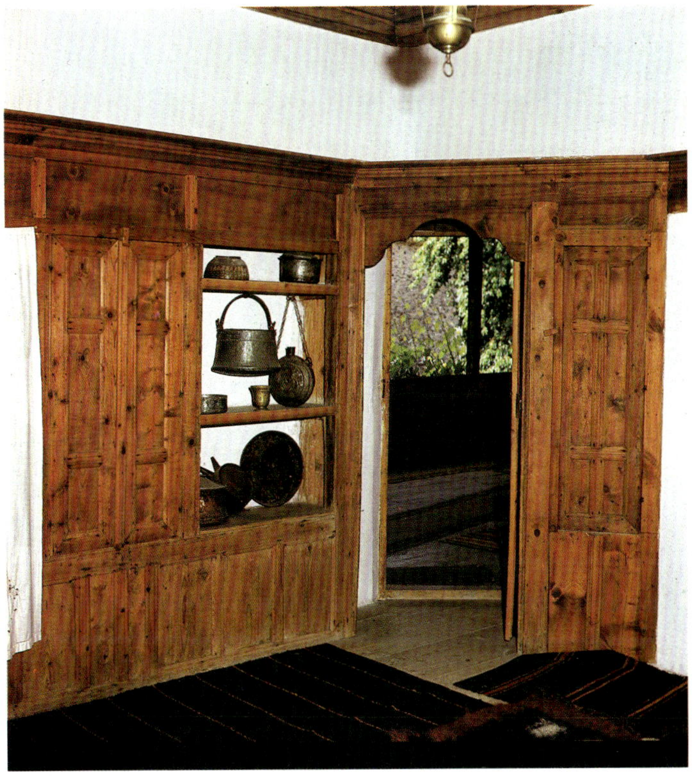

Wardrobe and place for water vessels (vodnik), Rhodope mountains.

predominantly rural, traditional house gradually began to comprise at least three principal rooms. The most important, and at the same time the largest of them, was the room with the fireplace, called *Kushta* or *Kushti*, in which all household jobs were performed in addition to its function as a dining-room and bedroom. The second room was the *soba* or *odaya* which was always connected to the first room. Initially it was not heated and was used for various domestic functions and as a storeroom, newlyweds and the younger members of the household often going to sleep there. Later, more windows were made in this room and it became the best room in the house in which guests were received. The pantry was the third most important room in the house. It was small, unheated and unlit, situated next to the room with the fireplace, and used to store food, household utensils and tools.

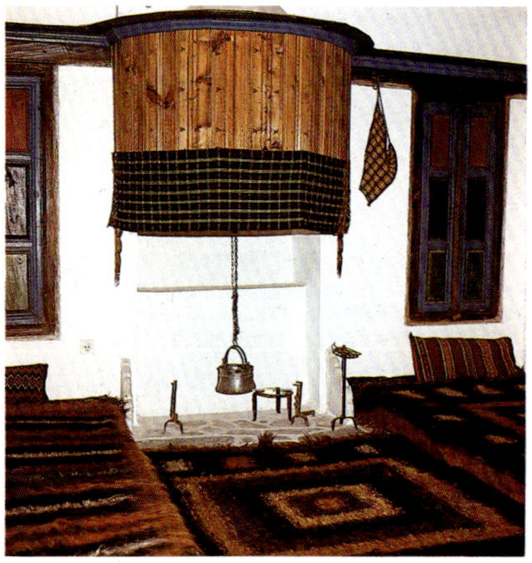

Room interior showing fireplace and goat-hair rugs, Rhodope mountains.

An essential element of the traditional Bulgarian house, (both functionally and as an architectural decorative solution) is the covered space or verandah which was totally or partially opened towards the courtyard, referred to as *proust*, *chardak*, *odur*, *sayvant*, *otvod*, or *poton*, in different parts of the country. It was always on the main facade of the house and many of the household activities took place there during the warm months. With the historical evolution of the house, this space acquired additional communicative and decorative functions in shaping the outer appearance of the house.

The increasing complexity of the plans followed two directions. First, the division of the principal rooms and the addition of new rooms in the direction that is at right angles to the line of entry, firmly establishing the rectangular shape of the house with one of the long walls as its main facade. Secondly, development of the structure in depth along the line of entry with the new rooms built in front and behind the room with the fireplace.

The increased number of rooms in the house was naturally accompanied by the enrichment of their functions. Additional spaces became functionally differentiated e.g. for making bread, clothes closets, storerooms, granaries, hiding places, and bathrooms. This process was most prominent in the house from the National Revival period, where the construction of the new rooms followed the two directions mentioned and resulted in houses having many rooms and elaborate plans, corresponding to the new standards of living and the social and cultural needs of the Bulgarian family during the National Revival period.

An important characteristic feature of the traditional Bulgarian house was its link with the courtyard and with the various farm buildings in it, as well as the organisation of its own functional accomodation. In the rural areas, in the plains, the farm buildings, including the stables and sheep pens, were initially situated next to the living quarters. In the mountains a vertical differentiation was followed: the ground floor usually served for the domestic animals, for cellars and other storerooms, while the upper floors provided the living quarters of the household. Since the 19th century, these archaic practices were gradually replaced by variants in which the domestic animals were already kept outside the house and the space originally intended for them was transformed into living space or used for various domestic or economic activities. With the development of artisan production, especially in the towns, these premises were frequently transformed into workshops, storerooms or shops. This introduced the practice of building the houses on the line of the street, with doors and shuttered windows opening towards the street so that the merchandise could be taken out and clients welcomed.

In the historical evolution of the traditional Bulgarian house specialists provisionally differentiate several basic house types. The longest persisting form among

Interior passage on the second floor of a traditional house.

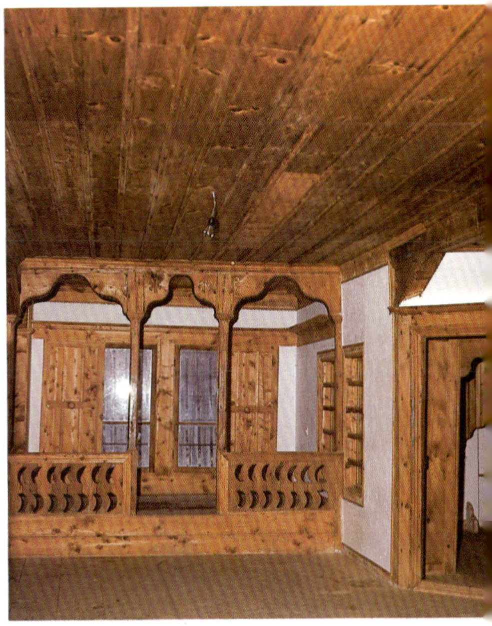

the oldest types of houses was the so-called *uzemna kushta* (one-storeyed building) partially dug into the ground and common along the Danube river in Northern Bulgaria. Other houses with a markedly horizontal silhouette are the *shopska* house typical of West-Central Bulgaria, and the houses from Dobroudja, Thrace and Strandja regions. The house from Central Bulgaria was most widespread: it was built on a raised stone plinth, having two or more storeys above it. Its varieties are known as the Tryavna, Teteven, Zheravna, Koprivshtitsa houses. Specific architecture can also be detected in the houses from the mountainous regions of the Rhodopes and Pirin. The architecture of houses in Bulgarian towns during the National Revival period, notably Plovdiv, Turnovo, Melnik, also betrays its peculiar characteristics.

The traditional house was erected by local builders with the active participation of the owners. It was the owner who determined the size and the appearance of the house, drawing on local tradition. With the intensification of the country's economic life in the 18th and 19th centuries building became an important means of livelihood for many settlements and regions. For example, builders from Tryavna and Gabrovo regions built houses all over central, north-eastern and south-eastern Bulgaria, builders from Trun made the houses in and around Sofia, especially to the south-west, while the builders from the Rhodope region were active in Aegean Thrace.

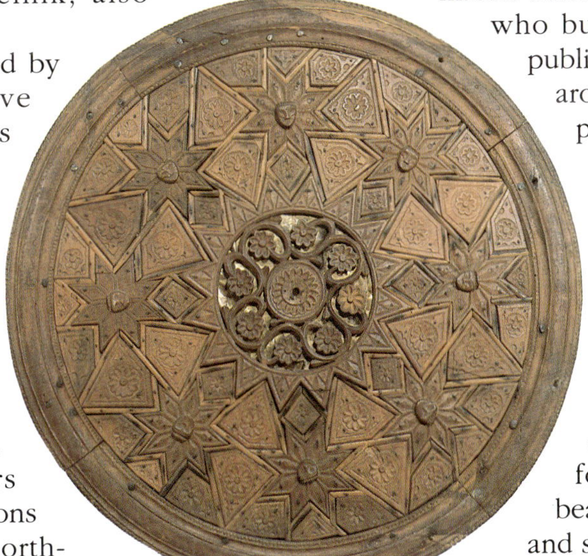

Ceiling, 19th Century, Sliven.

Bulgarian builders were universal specialists. They used traditional Bulgarian measures, they were familiar with the centuries-old Bulgarian building practices and made everything themselves: the stone masonry, the wooden structures, the fixed interior decoration elements - fireplaces, built-in cupboards, ceilings, sofas, shelves, and naturally the plastering of the walls, the door and the window frames. The best among them were also experts in the art of woodcarving and they decorated columns, doors, parapets, window-sills and other parts of the house. They never left their names on the houses they built, but the competence of the best made them widely known. A notable example in this respect is the self-taught master-builder Kolyu Ficheto from Dryanovo, who built remarkable churches, inns, public buildings and fountains in and around Turnovo, even defeating a professional engineer in a competition for the building of a large stone bridge with fourteen arches at Lovech in the second half of the 19th century.

The large-scale construction which spread in Bulgarian lands during the National Revival period, the evolution of a specific Bulgarian personality for towns and villages, with the beautiful houses, picturesque streets and squares with clocktowers, became one of the many spheres in which the young Bulgarian nation expanded its creative potential.

Let us enter one of the traditional Bulgarian houses from Central Balkan Range region (partially reconstructed and displayed in the Liverpool Museum 1989 Exhibition). The house strikes the eye with its white-washed walls and its surround of potted plants and flowers.

A wooden staircase will lead you up to the open-air verandah which is decorated with beautiful columns,

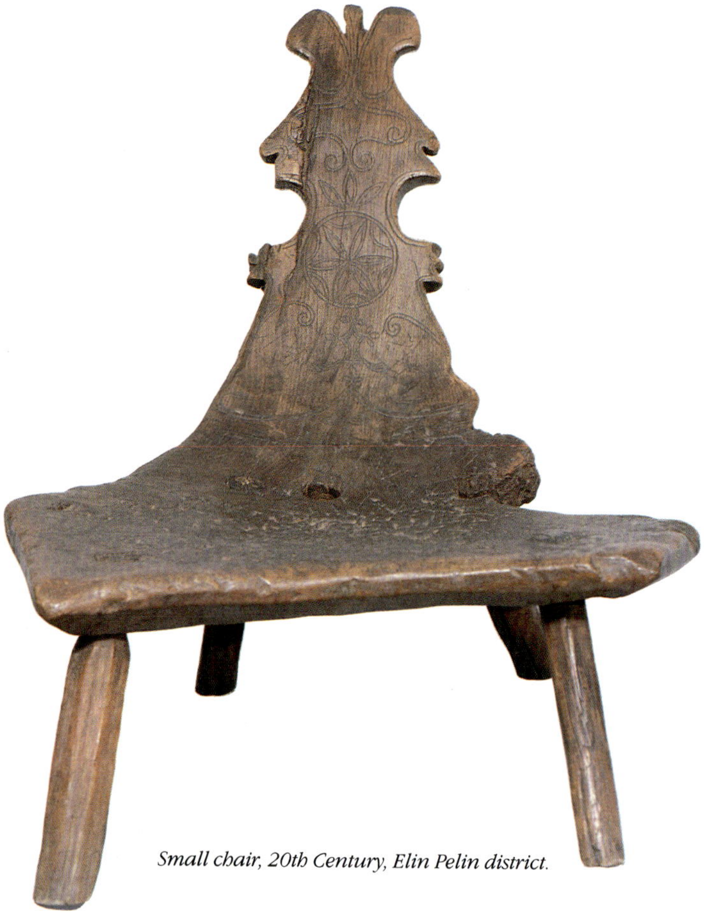

Small chair, 20th Century, Elin Pelin district.

with a beautiful view around. The vcrandah leads directly to the large room with the fireplace in the centrilateral corner to the door. This is the principal room of the house - *Kushti.* If the lady of the house does not invite you to pass directly into the adjacent room for receiving guests and if you happen to stay in the big room a little longer, you will understand quickly the rationality and simplicity of its organisation. The cauldrons, the water-jugs for fresh water and various other household vessels are kept in the *vodnik* - a type of dresser to the right of the entrance. Behind it are the wooden box for the flour and the trough for kneading bread. Almost the entire opposite wall is occupied by built-in cupboards in which food, vessels, bedclothes, blankets and clothes are kept. A fire is burning in the fireplace and food is cooked there. The table laid in front of the fireplace suggests that the entire household take their meals there. Various small objects are placed in niches around the fireplace. This centuries-old practice has determined the place of every object, as well as the positions and the functions of each member of the household. The most frequently used vessels are usually placed on shelves on both sides of the fireplace.

The observant visitor cannot help noticing the few items of mobile furniture: the table, the stools and some other domestic utensils, which are easily moved and make it possible to adapt the room quickly to the requirements of various other activities, for example: housework, cooking eating, looking after the children, and sleeping.

To the left of the fireplace, on the eastern wall is the inconostasis with the icon. A lamp is placed on a small window next to the door leading to the adjacent room so that it can throw light into both rooms simultaneously. Also very impressive is the ingenious use of vertical space. Although the room has no special ornamentation, it is nevertheless pretty and cosy. The visitor is attracted by the multicoloured rug on the floor, the discrete woodcarving on the doors of the cupboards and the decorated bowls and dishes on the shelves. Even the dark wood of the beams on the ceiling are in beautiful contrast to the white-washed walls and the soft glow of the polished copper vessels. This is what the main room in the traditional Bulgarian house looked like and this is where most of the indoor life of the family took place.

However, the hospitable host will not leave you for long to look around and will hurry to take you to the next room - the *soba* - where guests are received. You are impressed by the festive atmosphere in it, produced by the colourful textiles and the beauty of the room. Along the walls with windows there is a long narrow divan with attractive cushions on which you will be invited to sit. In front of this divan and all over the floor there are various rugs, carpets and fleecy blankets. Clay and copper vessels again glow on a beautifully carved shelf above the windows. Among these vessels one can spot souvenirs brought from

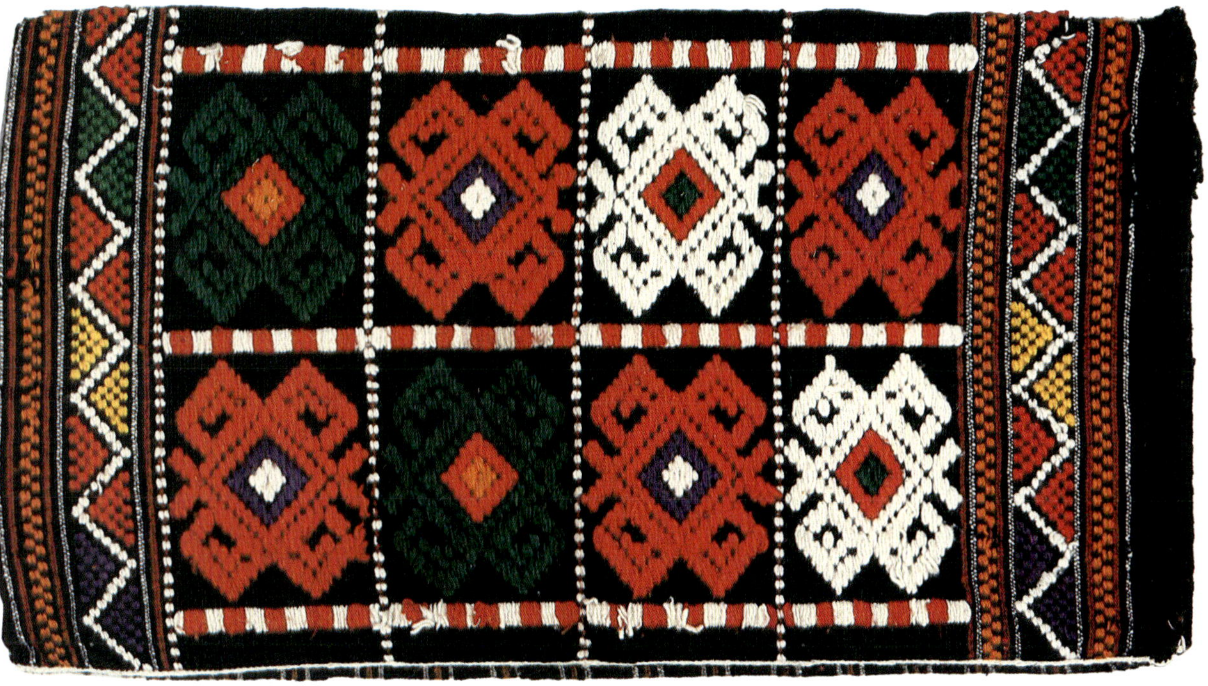

Cushion, early 20th Century, Silistra district.

travels to remote fairs and from distant lands like Wallachia, Russia, Austria-Hungary, or imported from abroad. Your eyes will no doubt be attracted by the ceiling rose which is exquisitely carved from wood. This represents the shining sun which is a symbol that occurs frequently in the Bulgarian house.

The guest-room is heated by a stove made of bricks, often whitewashed, which is connected to the adjacent room where the fire is lit. It is made in many local variants, each of which has its unique beauty and harmony of the proportions. Next to the stove there is a wooden chest on which textiles are piled. This is part of the dowry of the lady of the house which she brought with her as a new bride to her husband's home. Here in the guest-room, you would be treated to a splendid meal or at least, depending on the precise occasion, offered home-made drinks with appetisers or coffee.

This main room in the house is also very rationally furnished. Its walls also often abound with built-in cupboards, with pretty wooden carved patterns on them, and in which various domestic items are kept. Innovations in the traditional house have also developed from this room. It was here that the first imported factory-manufactured objects were introduced such as vessels, mirrors, tables, chairs, candelabra, and curtains.

Textiles played a very important role for the interior decoration of the traditional Bulgarian Home. The floor was covered with multicoloured rugs and carpets, the divans with fleeced rugs and cushions, while embroidered towels and curtains were hung round the windows and on the mirrors. The traditionally white walls of the houses from the National Revival period were painted and even decorated with plant and geometric motifs in the houses of the more affluent Bulgarians. Decorated, vaulted niches with various ornamentation (*alafranga*) appeared in the main rooms, generally between the built-in cupboards or doors, and decorative objects such as vases of flowers and mirrors, were placed in these niches.

There is a great variety in the interior decoration of the traditional and National Revival Bulgarian houses and in their architectural design and planning. This resulted from the original development of the numerous local and regional variants, which gradually but firmly established the unity and variety of the Bulgarian home as a type of living environment. In all cases, however, it was characterised by simplicity and convenience, as well as by the lack of unnecessary demonstrativeness and extravagance.

The house, the main material asset of the family, provided protection and the means of raising children. It was built in the course of the entire human life. The housewife invested in it all her most profound feelings and emotions, all her most cherished aspirations towards beauty, happiness and well-being. This has made the Bulgarian home so comfortable and cheerful that once the visitor enters, they may wish to stay for a long time.

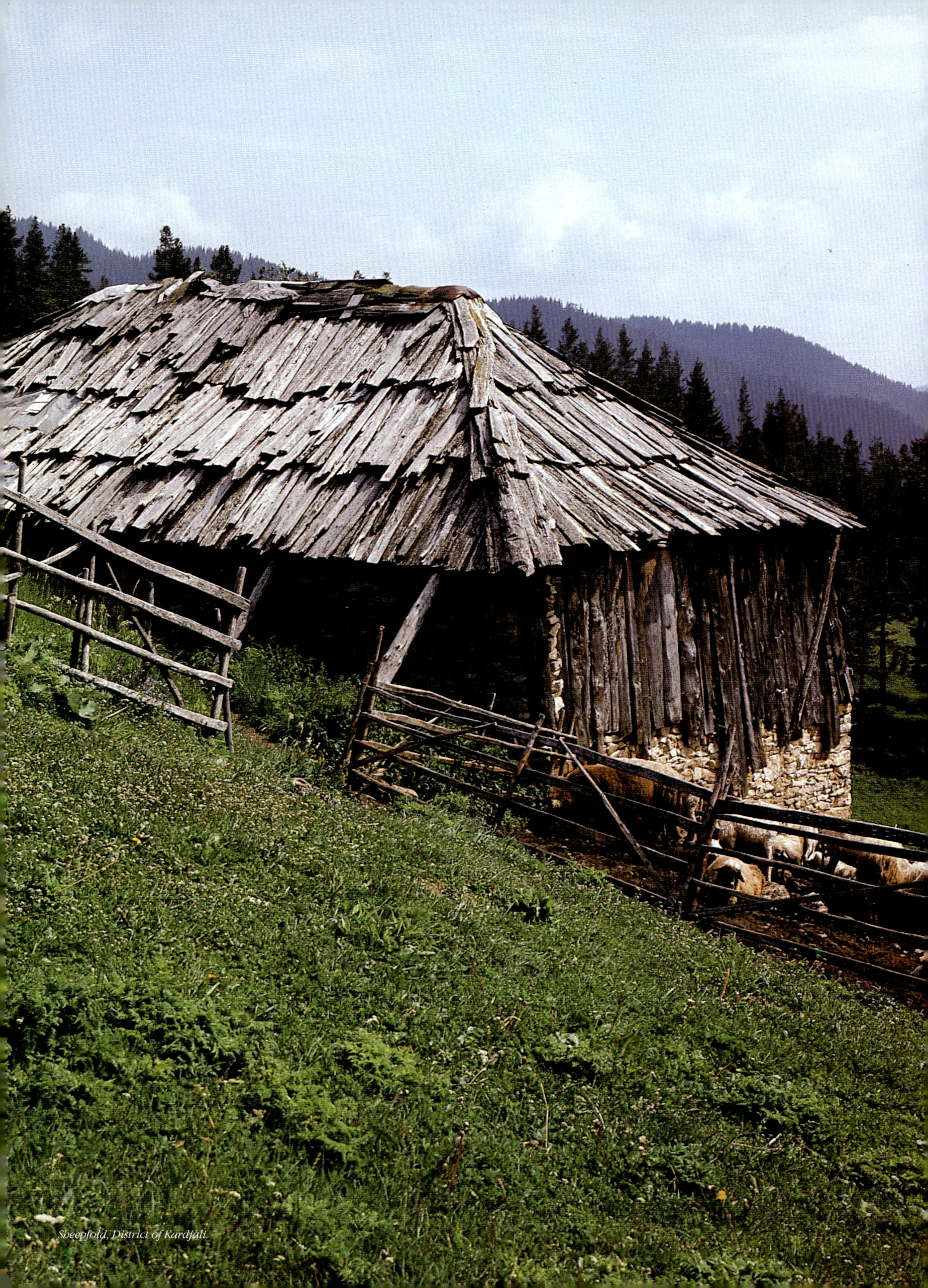

Sheepfold, District of Kardjali.

Shepherding

Ivan Kraynov

Homer in his work of genius "The Iliad" used to call ancient Thracia "mother of sheep". On Greek vases from the classical period there are pictured Thracians in hooded cloaks ("yamourloutsi") of a kind which are still worn by the Bulgarian shepherds.

The Slavs and ProtoBulgarians in particular also came to these lands with experience in cattle-breeding and their skill is intermingled with the ancient local tradition. Many Byzantine, Arabic and other chroniclers provide accounts of highly-developed stockbreeding after the foundation of the Bulgarian nation. The Arabic writer Al-Masoudi notes in the 10th century that "all give-and-take as well as marriage agreements are performed by means of bulls and sheep". The written records of the time of the First and the Second Bulgarian State (7th to 14th century) are a testimony of this means of living.

In spite of the decline of economic life in the early years of Ottoman rule, stock-breeding remained an important method of earning one's living. A substantial part of it belonged to shepherding which was highly-developed in the period between the 15th and 19th century. The needs of the Ottoman army and the large consumer centres of the Empire brought on its rapid development. A separate social category was introduced "djeleptchii" or shepherds and merchants. The greater part of them were Bulgarians and their job was to supervise the delivery of small farm animals. As early as the first half of 16th century about 3,700 registered Bulgarian "djelepi" (cattle-drovers) delivered 130,000 head of sheep.

As was the case in Britain for a certain period of time, shepherding in the Balkans became the primary source of earning a living and of providing such basic necessities as milk, dairy products, meat, leather and wool.

In the skilful hands of Bulgarian women the wool turned into beautiful textiles which were used either in the house interior or sold at the markets and the fairs throughout the Ottoman Empire. A number of foreign travellers and diplomats noted the high quality of the Bulgarian fabrics and their success at the market. Weaving gradually grew from a domestic occupation into a craft and then served as a basis for the manufacture of woollen textiles. Raw wool and leather became the main export articles in the trade of merchants from Doubrovnik, Venice and other places.

The demand for sheep and sheep by-products in the 18th to 19th century intensified, leading to a further flourishing of shepherding in the regions of Kotel, Koprivstitsa, Panagjurishte, and the central part of the Rhodopes. A great number of small farm animals were raised in the rest of the Bulgarian lands. The Bulgarian population became a main supplier of milk, dairy products and meat for all big towns. In this way shepherding became an essential factor for the development of manufacture and trade, for the accumulation of capital and the establishing of a capitalist type of economy in these lands, the same phenomena being observed in Britain as well.

The forms and the methods of shepherding in the various regions are, however, not the same. In those regions where agriculture was the main way of life sheep have been raised mainly for personal needs, and on the village land. They were either tended by one or more members of the family or a common flock was formed, gathering together the sheep of close relations or neighbours with a village boy or a shepherd being hired to pasture them.

The vast fields in Dobroudja and Thrace and the lush pastures high in the mountains provided the background for the development of large scale mobile shepherding concerns. The enormous flocks were constantly provided with pasture and leaf fodder from the woods. Many shepherds from the Rhodopes, Strandja, Sredna Cora, Pirin, and Galichnik in southwest Bulgaria descended from the mountains with their flocks and went in August to Thrace or East Thrace where pasture was available throughout the winter, due to the milder climate. Shepherding in the Rhodopes declined after the Balkan wars when the pastures of the Aegaen region were closed to the Rhodope shepherds

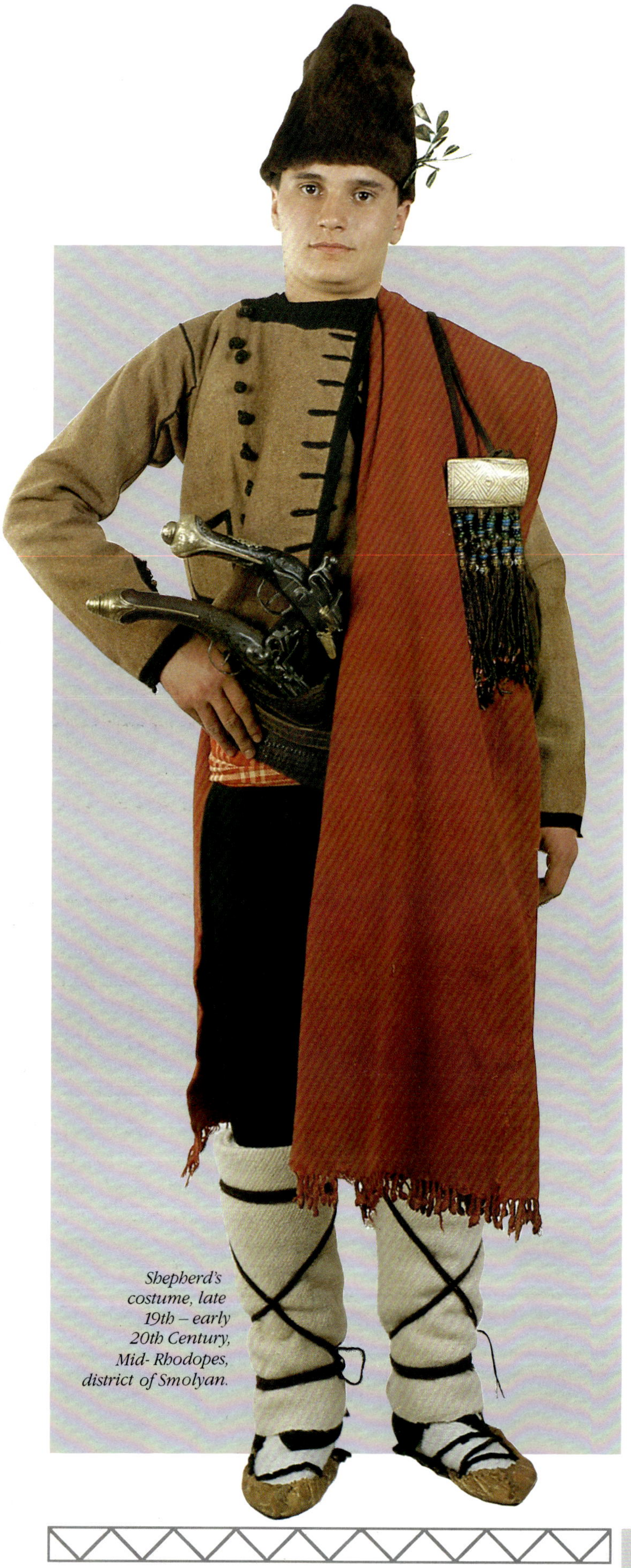

Shepherd's costume, late 19th – early 20th Century, Mid- Rhodopes, district of Smolyan.

because of the unbearably high fees for crossing the frontier. The shepherds from the region of Kotel moved instead to North Dobroudja and the total number of their animals was estimated at 450,000 head of sheep.

With large mobile shepherding concerns came more complex problems. Several common flocks of one or two big owners or those of a few smaller ones were formed. In most of the cases the co-operative was headed by a rich owner who hires a chief shepherd. Chief shepherds were chosen from among experienced, reliable, fair and prosperous shepherds, as they had the highest rights and obligations. The main owner was obliged to provide winter pasture and pens for the sheep and to pay the shepherds their wages. When the co-operative was formed by small owners the chief shepherd, who was also a contractor, took care of everything and was responsible for settling all the expenses.In turn the Chief shepherd hired other shepherds as well as a man (usually a dairyman) who provided them with food. In summer temporary workers were hired for shearing the sheep, and for building light shelters in the fields.

The usual places for housing the sheep in winter are the sheep-pens. These vary in their construction and in their numerous local names depending on their location. Alongside the pens, huts are usually erected for the shepherds to take shelter and in which to keep their equipment. The pens for housing the sheep in summer are lighter and can be easily moved to village lands. They go together with mobile huts which are put on runners or wheels to be easily removed. The sheep-pens and huts are constructed by the shepherds themselves.

The way of life of shepherds is determined by the nature of their job. In the Bulgarian lands the keeping of sheep is one of the basic means of living, and the prestige of the people performing this difficult activity has traditionally been high. Their typical characteristic is the highly developed professional disposition. Former or present they have always been proud of their occupation. The title "honorable chief shepherd" given to the Rhodope shepherds has always been

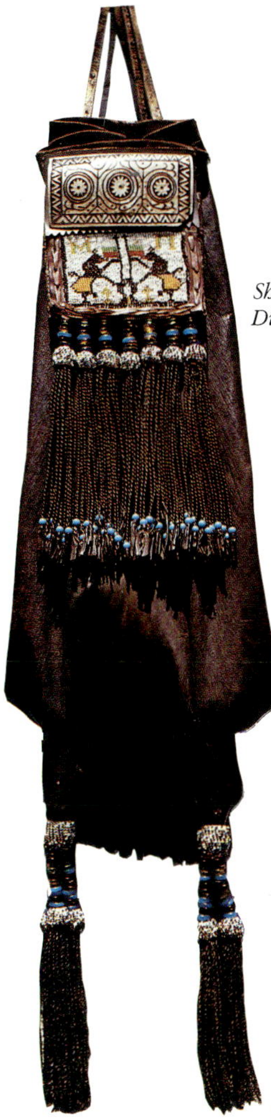

Shepherd's sack, District of Devin.

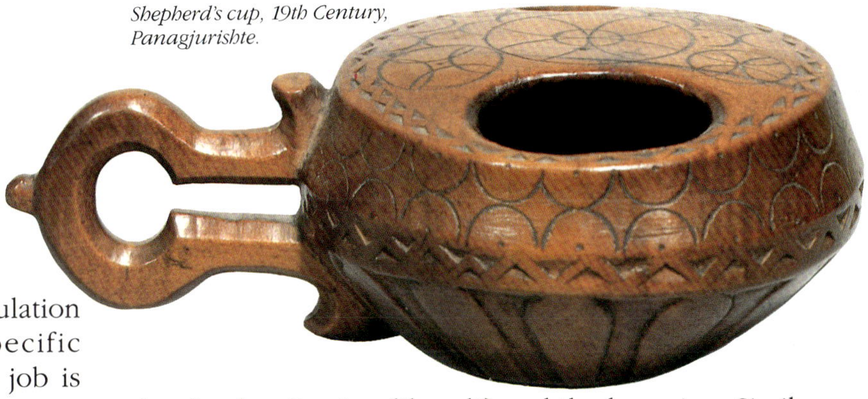

Shepherd's cup, 19th Century, Panagjurishte.

highly regarded by the population in those areas. The specific character of the shepherd's job is the reason for the distinctive character of their clothing. A typical garment is the hooded cloak "yamourlouk", which protects the shepherd from cold, rain and snow. In some regions other principal types of clothing are known including the red Rhodope scarves with fringes, the large hood "gougla", covering head and shoulders, and boots "nogavitsi", for protecting the feet from snow, rain and mud. Main accessories to the shepherd's clothing are the leather belt "siliah", the shepherd's bag and the cudgel. The "siliah" is made with several pockets for carrying pistols, silver cartridge-boxes and broad-handled knives, pouches with tobacco, flint and steel, and instruments for tending the sheep. The leather bags, decorated with tassels, beads and bone plates, are used for keeping the food fresh. Bag-pipes, shepherd's pipes and other objects can also be carried in these.

The large wooden vessels for keeping milk, churns, and wooden kegs for cheese, are made by coopers and the shepherds pay for them with the products of their labour. The metal kettles, the forged shears, the dog collars, are all made by skilful coppersmiths and blacksmiths. Shepherds hang cast and forged bells around the sheep's and goats' necks and enjoy the melodious toll, cast on the air. In the Rhodopes owners and shepherds compete in possessing the most tonal set of 12 cast bells. They are arranged in tonal order as a means by which they guess when the flock is returning from pasture. The musical instruments used by the Bulgarian shepherds for entertainment are the pipe, the shepherd's pipe ("kaval") and the bag-pipe. Similar bag-pipes are known in Scotland.

In their leisure time shepherds make wooden articles with a simple pen-knife to be used by them or their families. Despite the simplicity of the tool they succeed in making masterpieces of folk art. Some of these objects (distaffs, cowls and staffs) serve for presents which shepherds give to their sweethearts. Other articles which they make out of wood include cudgels, hooks, decorated sticks, shepherds' cups, salt-cellars, spoons and spoon-holders, all of them decorated by shallow wood-carving, called "herdsman's wood carving". This is distinguished by variable geometric motifs, vegetal, animal and human figures, related in some way to mythology.

The same ornaments can be found on powder-boxes, made of bone or horn, horns for keeping tar and bone plates used for decorating the shepherd's bag. An attractive feature of the "hooks" for the shepherd's clubs and staffs , cups and spoons are the beautiful patterns created by the amateur wood sculptor. The images carved in them are a reflection of their carver's ideas of the visible and invisible world. The specific mode of life of shepherds, their everyday communion with the magnificent Bulgarian landscape are sources of creative expression. The marvellous folk songs, the tunes of shepherds' pipes and bag-pipes, the harmonious toll of bells, the cudgels, cups and maidens' distaffs, decorated with wood-carving - are only a part of the spiritual treasure inherited from those of our forefathers who used to earn their living by shepherding.

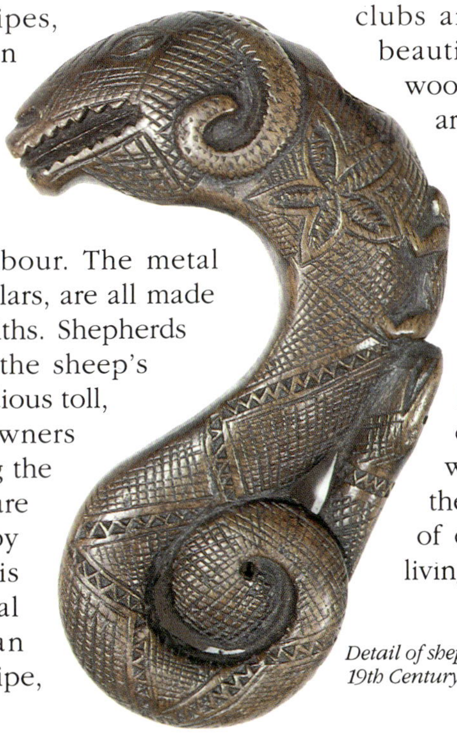

Detail of shepherd's crook, 19th Century, Pirdop district.

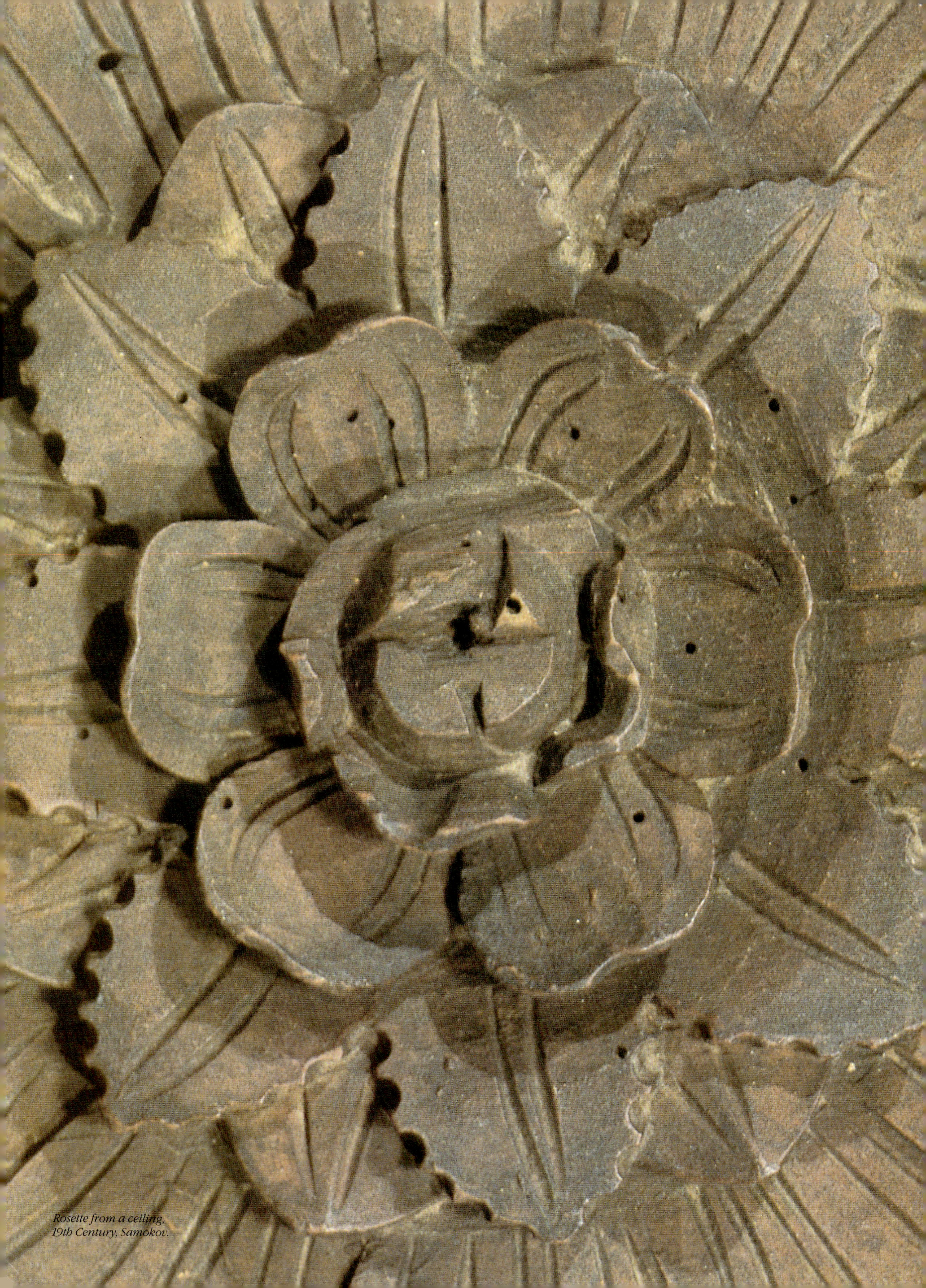

Rosette from a ceiling, 19th Century, Samokov.

Woodcarving

Silvia Vassileva

The architecture of the Bulgarian house demonstrates expedience and simple function but also it has amazingly rich and original decoration; this is mainly concentrated upon the facade and the interior. In the decorative design of the Revival house wall painting, wood-carving and the masterfully made details are generally included in the scheme. The artistic design of the premises is however, subjected to their basic function.

Wood-carving is an ancient and typical part of the Bulgarian folk art and one of its Slavonic components. It is inseparably connected with the wooden architecture which in the period of the Revival was already centuries old. The profusion and accessibility of the wooden material made it widely-used in building. It is suitable both for constructing and decorating the house. Being easy to work, wood is suitable for the creation of various articles and for richly embossed decoration. During the 18th and 19th centuries because of the expansion in building, wood-carving became a self-dependent folk craft and was developed in a number of schools in Tryavna, Debur, Kalofer, and Razlog. The schools differ in their techniques, depth and tracery of relief, preference for certain motifs and in their vivid, realistic or schematic treatment of human and animal figures.

The Revival master carvers clung to tradition but also actively sought out new forms and new means of expression, to give their works profound meaning and beauty. The pattern of carved wood of the Revival period is indicative of what was typical for the time, preserving at the same time some features whose origin can be found in the culture of the Middle Ages. The penetrating influences of some Eastern and European schools have generally been absorbed by the vivid artistic traditions existing in Bulgaria.

Carved wood and wall-painting were artistic means largely used in the decoration of the Bulgarian Revival house by the builders themselves who would take charge both of building and decorating the house. The location, the material and the carved wood motifs were chosen most carefully, obtaining great artistic effect with economy of materials. In most cases masters did not use pattern books but created their motifs while carving, according to the place and material. Secular wood-carving unlike church wood-carving lacks elaborate figured compositions. The interior decoration of the house is mainly based upon the rhythmic repetition of the same decorative elements, on the alternation of similar forms or combinations of a number of different motifs, close in form. Masters drew inspiration for their motifs

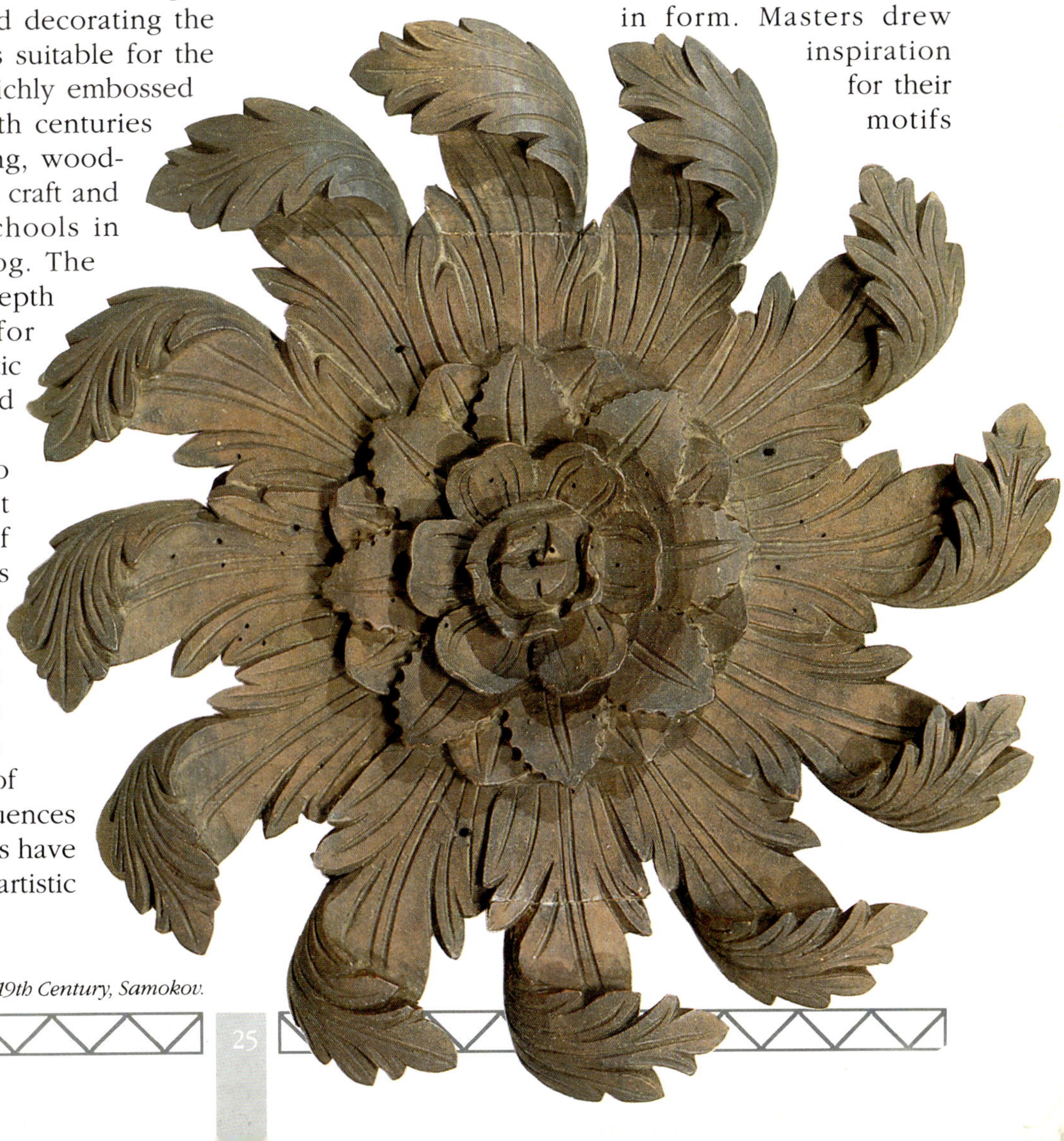

Rosette from a ceiling, 19th Century, Samokov.

from the beauty of nature. Much admired were those of roses, grapes, oak leaves, and flowers. A bright spring sun was usually carved in the ceilings.

Through artistic, though sometimes naive forms of compositions, reflecting the ideas, feelings and moods of the Bulgarian, carved-wood decoration and the decoration of the Bulgarian house exhibits optimism and joy and bears definite national features. It lacks pomposity and has intimate colouring.

Different techniques are applied in the wood-carving of the house. In some cases it is deep, embossed, even open-work with some ceilings and columns whereas in others it is more shallow, outlining only the silhouette of forms and motifs. The use of different kinds of wood (walnut, pear, pine, hazel, oak) leads to rich combinations of colours within the distinct elements of the interior, without becoming flamboyant.

Carved-wood decoration can be found everywhere about the house. First, visitors are met by the simple carved-wood elements on the gate. Then attention is drawn to the carved consoles of the verandah, the railings and the doors inside the house. Special attention was paid to carving the wood in the parlours.

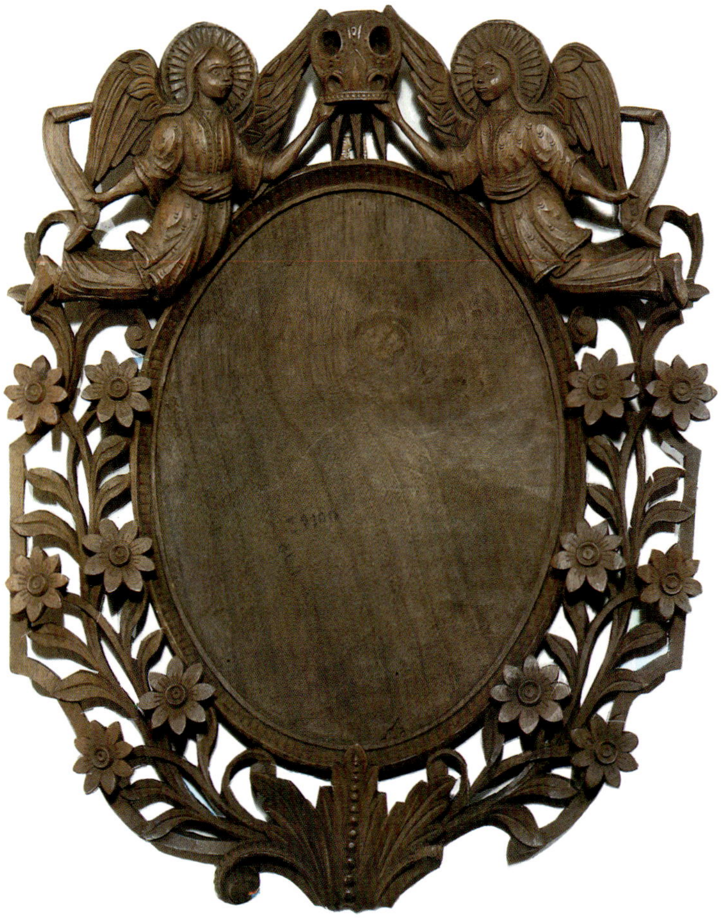

Mirror frame, 19th Century, Samokov.

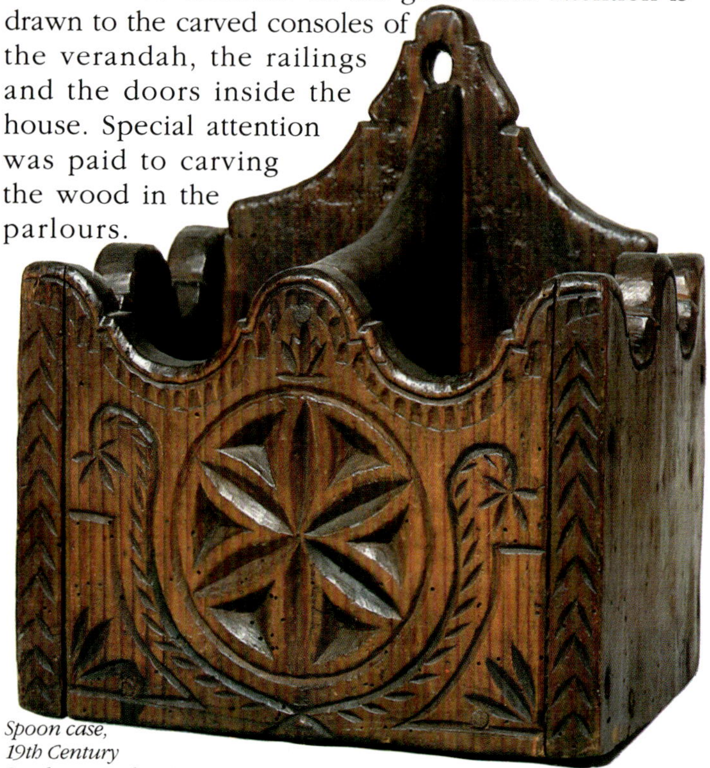

Spoon case, 19th Century South-west Bulgaria.

Highly significant for the decorative scheme is the treatment of the ceiling. Here can be seen most clearly the specific features of the different wood-carving schools in the country, indicated by the preferences for particular motifs, their place and composition. In the ceiling are carved geometrical figures, forming compositions. The centre of the composition may be a clearly-cut rosette, representing the sun. The friezes to it are ornamented with vegetal motifs, and bunches of

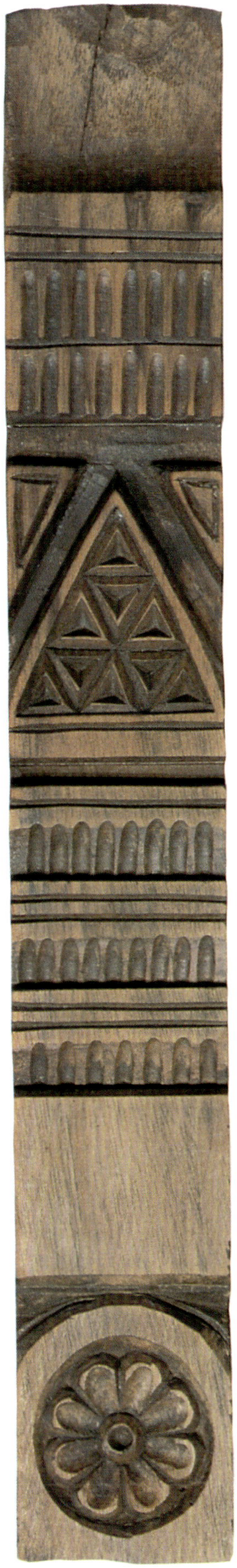

Console, 19th Century, District of Kotel.

flowers, all of them amazing in their harmony. In these carved forms can be seen the sense of harmony and beauty of the Bulgarian masters.
Carved-wood rosettes, stylised vegetal ornaments and geometrical figures can also be found on the doors of the built-in-closets. The wood-carving here is not so deep, neither is it on the friezes and shelves which make them all perfectly harmonious. The inconostases, columns and consoles have open-work carving of different structure. The carved forms are sculptural and three-dimensional.
The achievements of the woodcarvers are a large part of the Bulgarian ethnic heritage, and a source of creative inspiration for both the modern master carvers and amateurs, (the best of them being members of the Guild of the Masters of Folk Crafts). For them the art of wood-carving is a means of expressing individual ideas, concepts and capabilities.

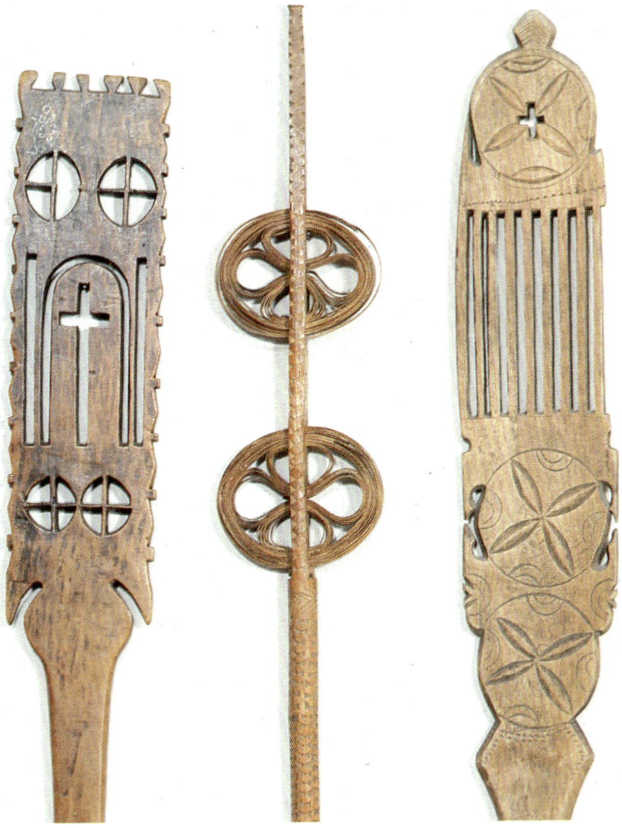

Wooden distaff from middle Bulgaria beginning of the 20th Century.

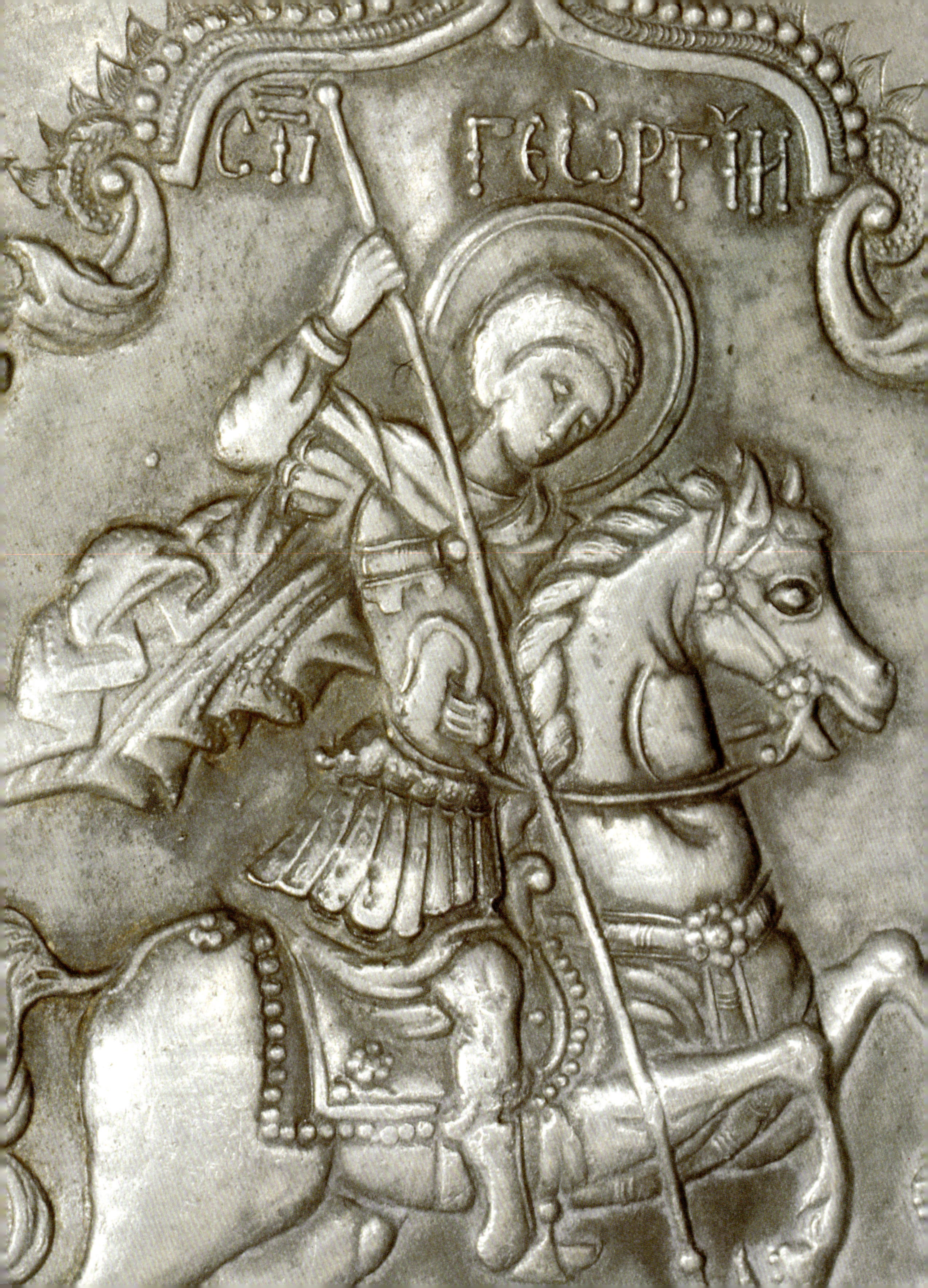
СТ ГЕѠРГІИ

Masters of Metalworking

Vyara Kovacheva – Kostadinova

Articles made of metal are a multi-faceted and significant part of the cultural and historical heritage of the Bulgarian people. As elsewhere the works made of ferrous and non-ferrous metals, as well as alloys, are created from a soil rich in minerals. Generations of known and unknown masters have made a variety of everyday items. Their patterns fully reflecting the people's concepts and ideas of beauty as an aesthetic expression of manners and moral standards.

The basis of the metalworking process is the traditions of the Thracians, Slavs and the ProtoBulgarians, as well as the cultural heritage of the Balkan countries themselves. Passed down through many generations is the sense of proportion and practicality in form and decoration. The material heritage which has been preserved, especially the articles made in the period of the National Revival are illustrative of the longevity of traditions in Bulgaria. They give us a chance to review periods of strong cultural relationship between this country and other countries of the world. They also reveal a kind of art, deeply syncretic in character, which has successfully withstood the historical vicissitudes and the oppression of political ideas upon the people and artisans.

The art of wrought copper is notable for the traditional preference of creating ancient, balanced silhouette forms, which are both pretty and functional. As a result of the creative abilities of the Bulgarian coppersmiths there appeared a great variety of household dishes and church and monastery plates. Centres of the craft were the mediaeval and the new-towns of the National Revival period. The dishes from Plovdiv, Ustovo, Sofia, Vidin, Karlovo, Shoumen and Stara Zagora were widely-sought in the market places of the Balkan countries. They were coveted things, ordered as gifts for monasteries, for newly married people, for newly-born babies, and for newly-built houses. The Bulgarian appreciates the durability and the beauty of the red wrought copper. Gifts are symbolic expressions of these ideas, and of good wishes for health and longevity.

This malleable, easily wrought metal was an ideal raw material for the development of ideas and capabilities. There was a great variety of copper dishes, with various usages, volumes and proportions. The dishes used for dining, such as bowls, jugs, mugs, cans, kettles for water, for wine or for cooking, baking-dishes and many other wrought-copper dishes were, and still are, an inseparable part of the interior of each Bulgarian house. The creation of forms of elaborate construction reveal perfect knowledge of the properties of the metal. A favourite creative manner is the stabilising hammering of the surface. The skill of choosing the right forging profile and rhythm of forging is unique. The elaborate combination of edging streaks and of dots of various sizes accentuates the details of form, and gives it a complete, natural and shiny beauty.

The surface decoration of the dishes strongly reflects the complex processes in the development of the Bulgarian coppersmith's craft under the influence of local, Balkan, and Mediterranean traditions, and of aesthetic views from the Orient and from the Near East. They put their impression on the decoration, by embossing or engraving. On the dishes can be seen forged triangles and lozenges, embossed rosettes, acanthuses, vegetal motifs, friezes or medallions with arabesque, figures of tulips, carnations, holly-hocks, all elaborately interlaced. The resonance of this ornamental manner in the work of the Bulgarian master is traditionally given a new meaning. There is nothing of the pomposity and luxuriance typical of the East. The compactness and the reckless repetition of motifs are missing, as well as the unnaturally pro-

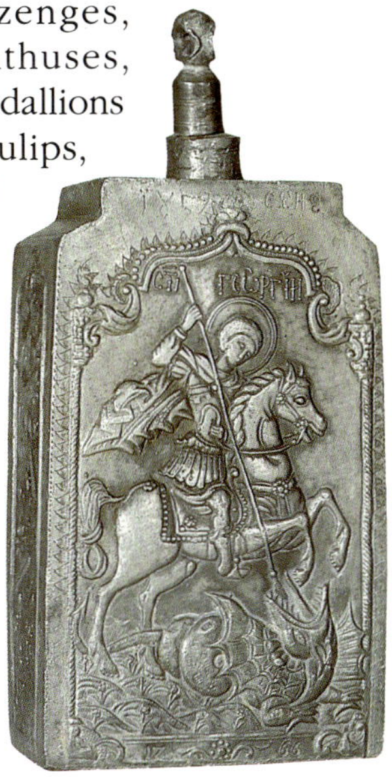

Brandy flask (lead), 1852, Troyan.

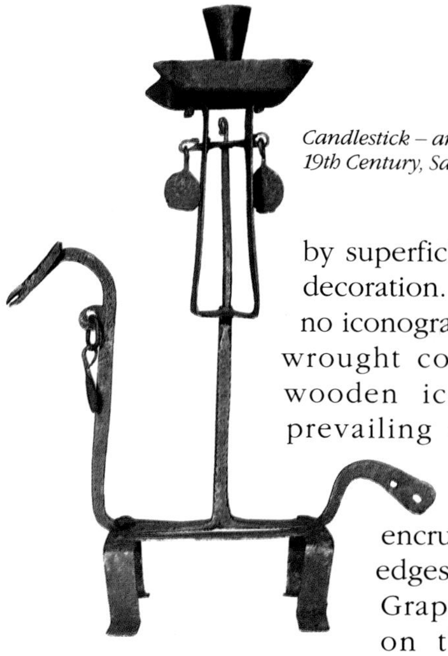

Candlestick – andiron, 19th Century, Samokov.

truding spouts, handles and necks of the dishes. The traditional sense of balance, and form, complemented by the decoration, has always been the predominant feature. It unites the craftsmanship of copper-smiths, potters, wood-carvers, and goldsmiths.

There hardly exists a craft as long lived, widely developed or more closely related to the everyday life of the Bulgarians than the traditional blacksmith's craft. Even in the days of the Revival when master goldsmiths, copper smiths and wood-carvers left their names on their works with the feeling of personal and national dignity the Bulgarian blacksmiths traditionally remained unknown. Their demanding job is a succession of different procedures; heating, forging, cutting off, filing, chaining or chopping of the solid black metal. From the craftsmen's hands there flowed to the market farming and craftsman's tools, articles of everyday life, architecture details, equestrian accessories, and arms. The hereditary blacksmiths from Samokov, Chiprovtsi, Kratovo, Gabrovo, and Etropole were outstanding. But it was not only purely utilitarian products that reached the customers. The functional properties of the iron-made articles was accompanied by superficial but deeply symbolic decoration. In them can be found no iconographic subjects, typical in wrought copper, and in carved wooden iconostases. Here the prevailing compositions are of streaks, dots, arcs, knots, fretwork, and encrustations. An ear of corn edges the curve of the sickle. Grapevines are carved out on the pruning-knife, a blade of grass on the ploughshare, or a fretwork rosette on the steel-yard. The selection of the motifs is a reminder of the article's function and of the ideas and intentions of both masters and farmers.

From this solid and hard-to-forge metal the most interesting patterns for fireplace accessories and magnificent church chandeliers have been created. The stylised, sculptured horse's head, one-horned serpent, bird, flower calyces and buds are indicative of exceptional mastership. Unique in design, in completeness of composition and rhythm is the fine geometrical or vegetal fretwork. It makes the body of the chandelier lighter, the trivet look exquisite, and the rosette-shaped gate handle a decorative feature. Thus in the blacksmith's craft practicality is allied with aesthetics, obliterating the boundary between craft and art.

There are various techniques in metal processing. The art of making dishes out of lead-tin alloy is a sign of a great skill in the casting of forms and in engraving. During 17th, 18th and 19th centuries, this craft flourished. In Troyan, Teteven, Samokov, Etropole, Sofia, and Prilep masters cast various things made to order: wine vessels, brandy flasks, and containers for keeping unction or holy water brought from Jerusalem. They were all of a small volume and bizarre form: flat, tetrahedral, hexagonal, round, or octahedral and worn at the waist-band. The miniature pitchers for coffee and sweet drinks were exquisite. The wine-vessels on fretwork stems, curved

Copper mug, 19th Century – beginning 20th Century, Vidin.

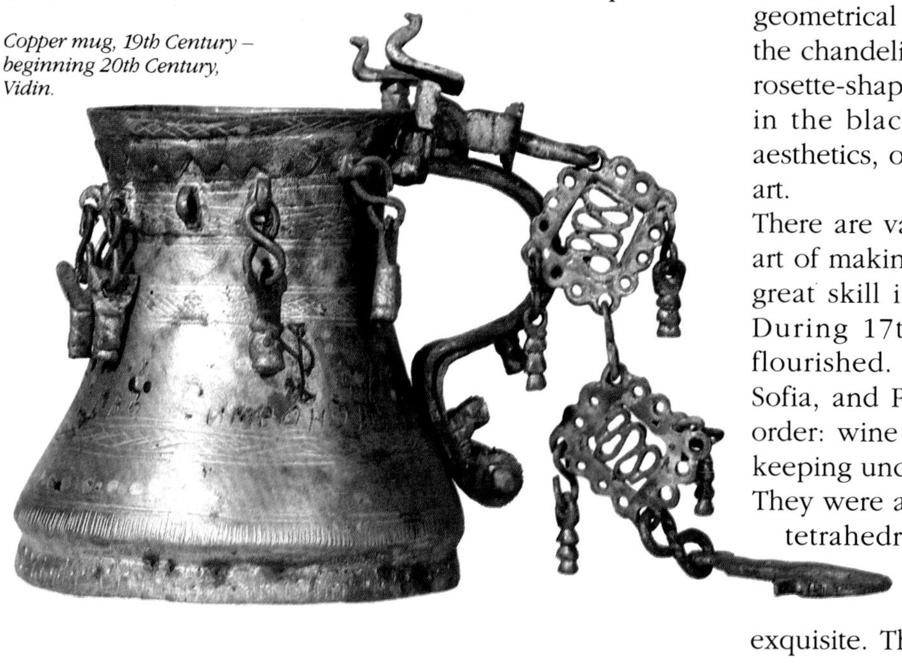

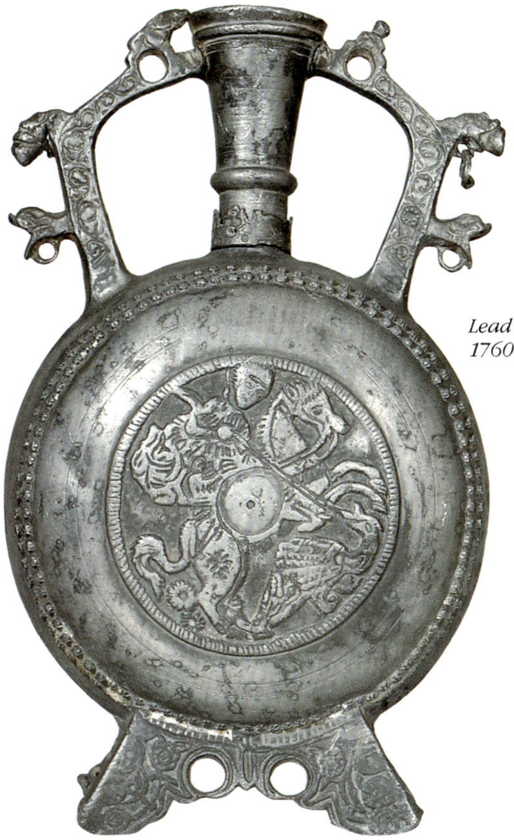

Lead vessel for holy water or wine, 1760, Plovdiv.

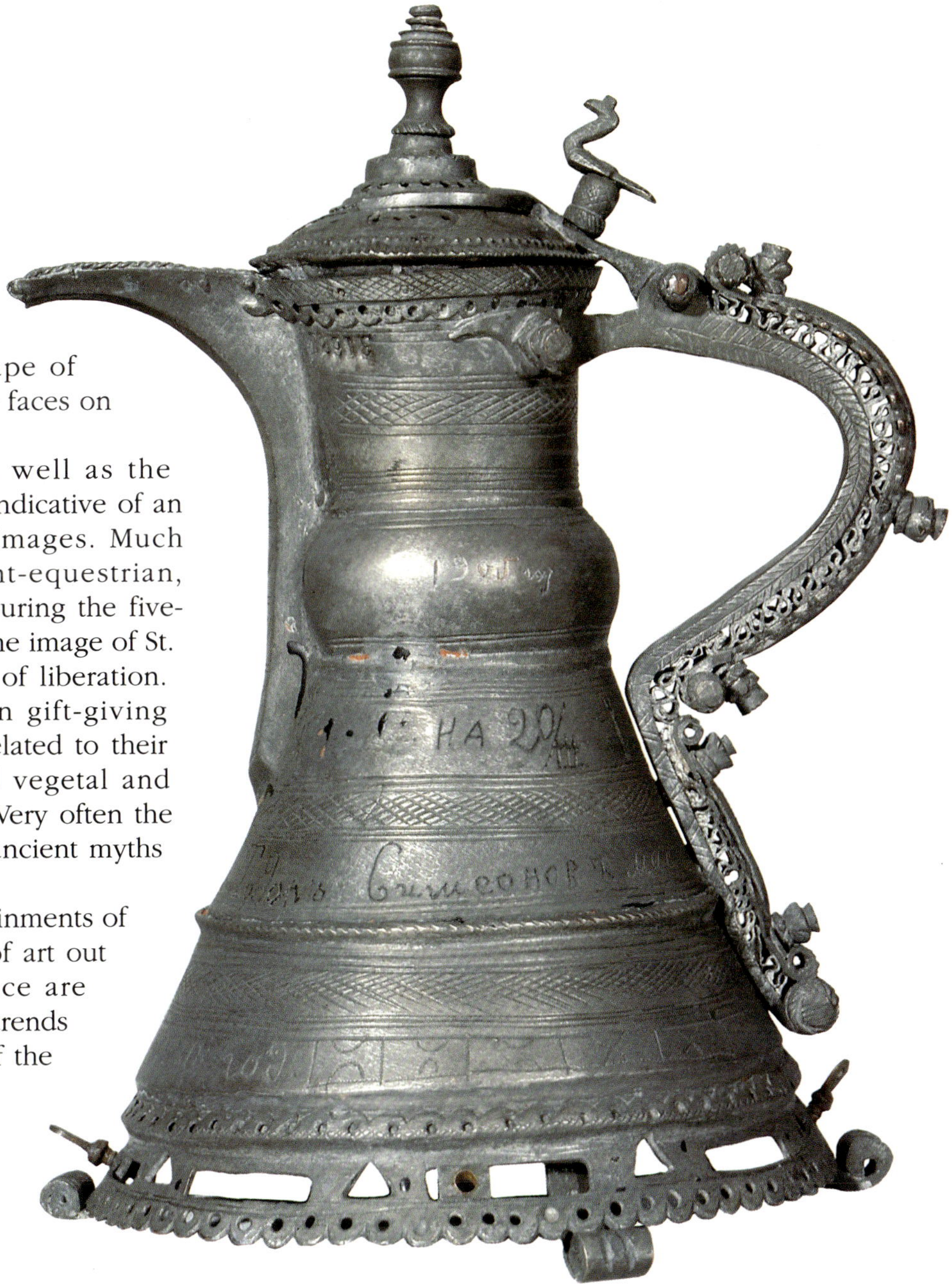

handles and projecting dragon's heads were equally beautiful and so were the brandy flasks in the shape of pigeons, fishes or with male and female faces on both sides.

The form of the casting mould, as well as the engraving on the embossed figure are indicative of an ancient tradition, rich in symbolic images. Much favoured are the images of the saint-equestrian, thrusting at a dragon with his lance. During the five-century period of Ottoman oppression the image of St. George became a symbol of the ideal of liberation. The lead-tin alloy vessels are rich in gift-giving inscriptions. Their function is closely related to their decoration. Geometrical and stylised vegetal and animal motifs complement each other. Very often the images and pictures used derive from ancient myths and biblical legends.

Still more could be added about the attainments of the traditional masters creating pieces of art out of metal. Their value and significance are intransient. In the syncretic mixture of trends and influences the originality of style of the Bulgarian masters reveals itself.

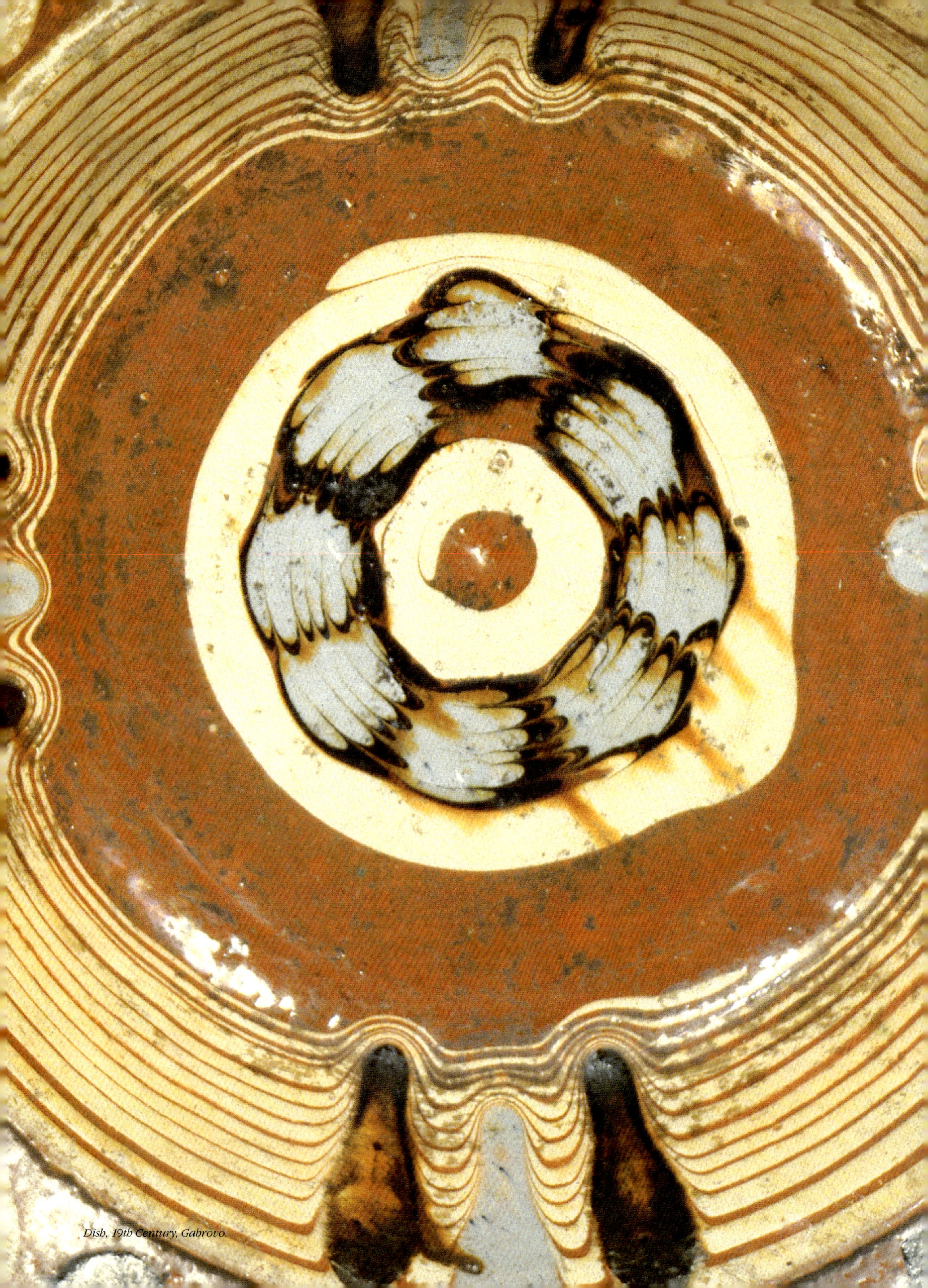

Dish, 19th Century, Gabrovo.

Ceramics

Emil Portalski

Bulgarian ceramics originated in the Thracian, Slavonic and Proto-Bulgarian traditions and as early as the Middle Ages (12th to the 14th century), its typical features were formed. The large amount of earthenware of varied forms and high aesthetic value which have been discovered is a testimony to the highly-developed potter's craft of those early periods. Since the end of the 14th century, the time when Bulgaria fell under Ottoman rule, traditional Bulgarian pottery began to decline. It lagged behind and was unable to maintain the high aesthetic value of the previous products.

The economic, social and cultural uplift in the period of National Revival favourably influenced the further development of folk crafts, including pottery. In most of the big towns potters' workshops emerged once more. Centres of pottery were gradually established which were and are of great importance to the development of pottery in the Bulgarian lands. The most significant are Boussintsi, Troyan, Gabrovo, Berkovitsa, Chiprovtsi, Razlog, Turgovishte, Teteven, Samokov, Pirot, Veles, Ressen, and Strouga.

Pottery in the Bulgarian lands is a typical folk craft. The masters hand down their skill to the younger generations. The seasonal work of potters in different parts of the country enables them to become acquainted with the various everyday as well as aesthetic requirements of people. This in itself leads to diversification of the range of earthenware. An important source for the enrichment and diversification of earthenware forms and decoration are the copper and lead tin vessels, church wood carving and mural paintings.

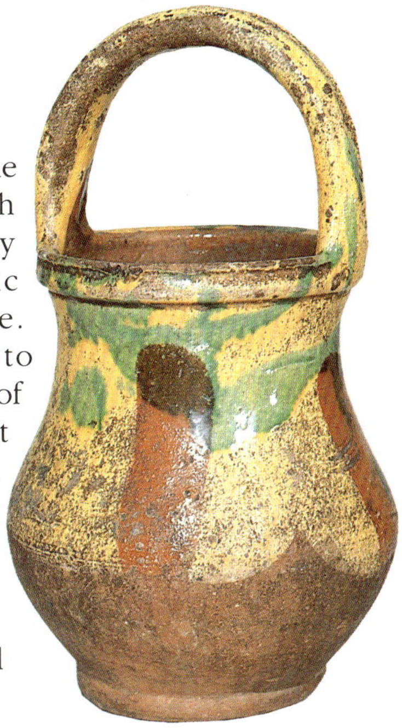

Ceramic pot (rakatka), 19th Century, Blagoevgrad.

In the large centres of pottery about 60 principal forms and more than 40 of their variants are used in the production of vessels to satisfy the multitude of needs and the aesthetic requirements of the population. Several groups of earthenware can be identified according to their function: *vessels* for keeping food and victuals (cans, jars, pots, vinegar bottles, butter dishes); *vessels* for preparing food (pots, baking dishes, pans, stew pots, colanders); *dining* dishes (pitchers, jugs, cups, bowls, plates, brandy flasks); *ritual* vessels (wedding pitchers, wine vessels, small kegs, bowls for boiled wheat, cups for holy water, baptismal fonts, censers, candlesticks); *vessels* for farm usage (tar vessels, smoke vessels and feeding troughs for bees, painter's cans, feeding troughs for chicken, covers and pots of cauldrons for boiling brandy, decorative tiles for fire-places, hoods for chimneys) and *articles* for personal usage, and decoration, etc (pipes, children's toys, safes, musical instruments, icons, vases, flower pots).

A characteristic feature of Bulgarian folk ceramics is the frugal ornamental design. Along with the opportunities offered by the various colours of the clay, potters used different techniques of decoration, among them being the pouring over with lead glaze coloured in yellow, green and brown. Decoration is not an end in itself. It

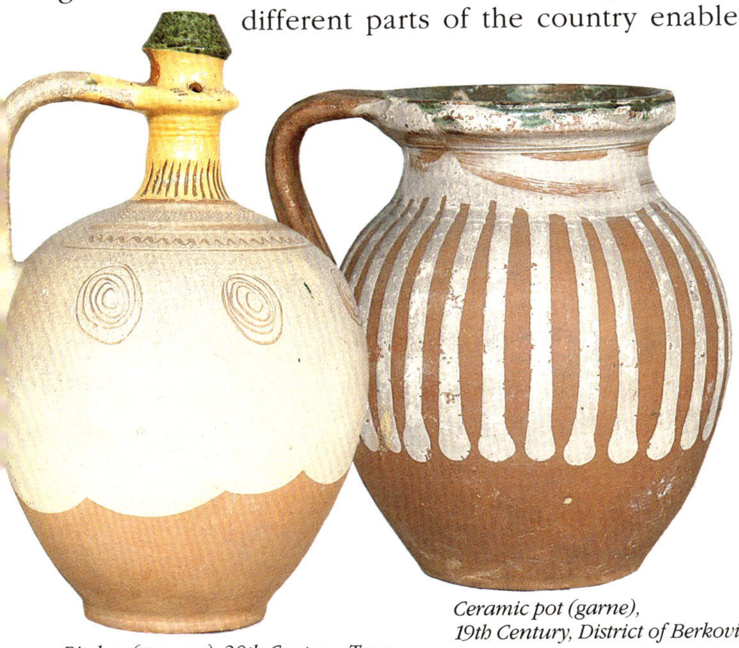

Ceramic pot (garne), 19th Century, District of Berkovitsa.

Pitcher (stomna), 20th Century, Trun.

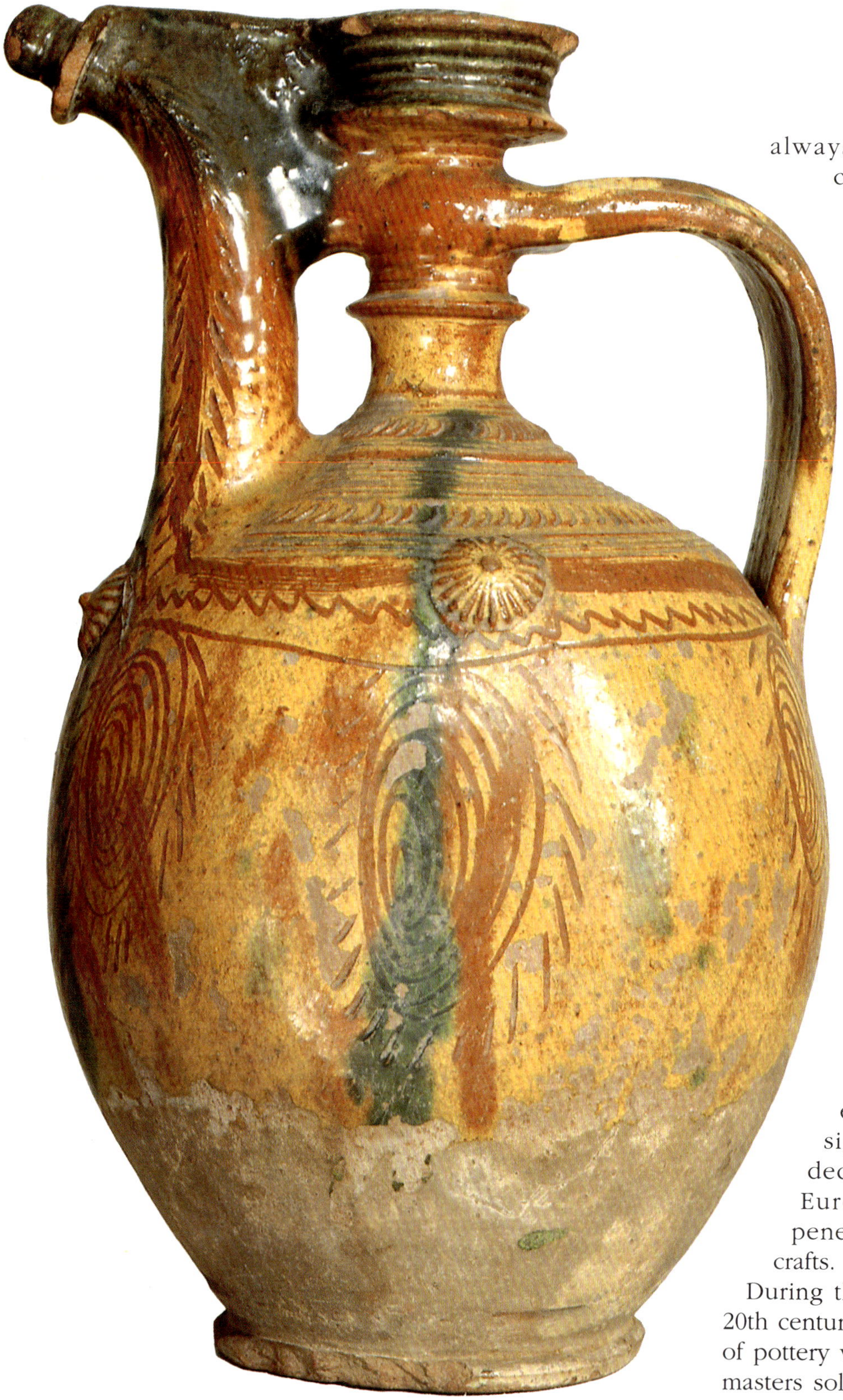

Pitcher (krondir), 19th Century, Boussintsi.

always matches the form of the product and complies with its function.

The old masters show high artistic skill in the decoration of the table-ware. The lead glaze, commonly used by them, with its transparent yellow colour tones down the contrast between the different colours of clay. The dark green oxide makes colours "sink", uniting them in pastel tonality. The motifs, mainly vegetal, and the colours seem to be taken from nature itself. It is not by chance that ceramic vessels, together with the variegated textiles, are the most colourful and lively part of the interior of the Bulgarian house.

Most ornate are the wedding pitchers and those called "krondir". Their florid decoration is due to their festive and ritual functions. They also play a significant part in the roles of their owners during the wedding ceremony.

It is not so much the form of the vessels as their variants and decoration that characterised the established centres of pottery in Bulgaria. These centres were of unparalleled significance. Some were very small local centres, others were of regional importance, and some others reached to up the level of manufacturing centres, marketing their products throughout the vast territory of the Turkish empire. They were of a different economic significance and at various times they all declined, unable to keep up with Western-European industrial manufacture, which penetrated into the Empire, ruining the local crafts.

During the 19th century and the beginning of the 20th century the most powerful and influential centres of pottery were Boussintsi and Troyan. The Boussintsi masters sold their products and did seasonal work in

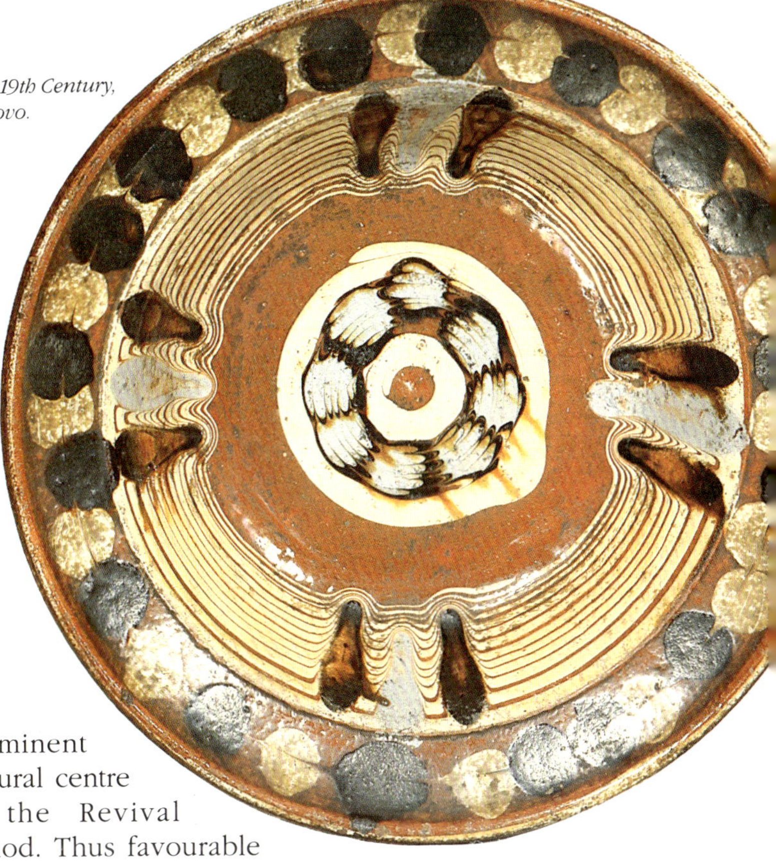

Dish, 19th Century, Gabrovo.

the West and South of Bulgaria, exerting influence over the pottery centres in these regions. The Troyan potters spread their production and influence mainly in the North and East of Bulgaria.

The style of the Boussintsi masters suggests an archaic origin of the product. Here the accent is put on the form. The profiles of many vessels are related to ancient epochs and some of them are perfect replicas of original ancient specimens. The ancient traditions find expression in the techniques used in the decoration of vessels, having as a base the Old Slavonic techniques of shallow-carved ornamentation. Throughout all periods of its development the Boussintsi ceramics preserve the pastel colours which makes the house look warm and comfortable. For this reason it was widely sought both in the villages and in the towns of West and South Bulgaria.

The Troyan ceramic school developed as the product of an outstanding manufacturing centre which acted as a trade centre as well, being situated along the main highway. It was also influenced by the Troyan Monastery, a prominent cultural centre in the Revival Period. Thus favourable conditions were established for the development of pottery. As early as the mid 19th century the Troyan masters made vessels of varied forms serving equally well both village and urban styles of life. The "urbanisation" of folk ceramics was typical of all Revival centres to a greater or lesser extent but is most conspicuous in the Troyan ware. Its specific design and pattern of decoration prove to be highly suitable for meeting the increasing requirements of consumers. That is why it was accepted by other centres of pottery, gradually beginning to possess a pan-Bulgarian character and to be identified as the national style.

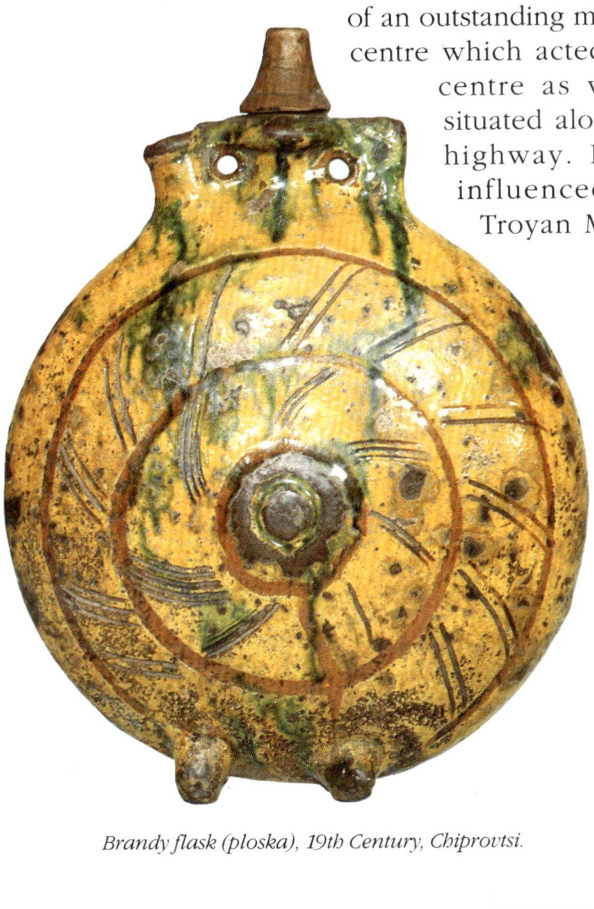

Brandy flask (ploska), 19th Century, Chiprovtsi.

The Liberation of Bulgaria from Ottoman oppression and the establishment of capitalist systems of production, leading to a flooding of the market with industrial goods, did not prove as destructive for pottery as it did for many other crafts in Bulgaria. The high artistic value of the vessels created by the Boussintsi and Troyan masters secured the vitality and existence of these two centres of ceramics as late as the 1930s and their qualities bring inspiration to today's practitioners.

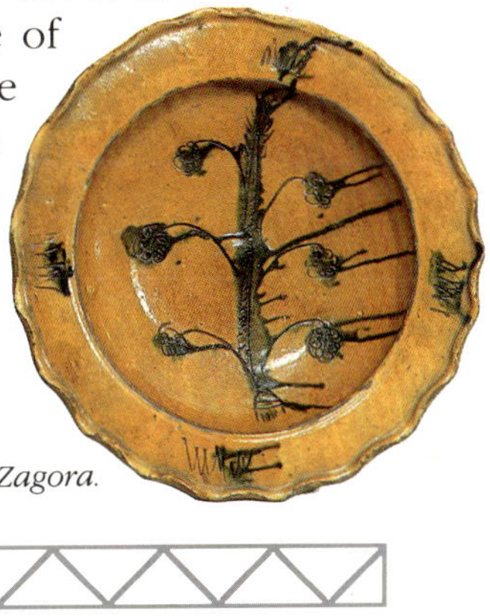

Dish, 19th Century, Stara Zagora.

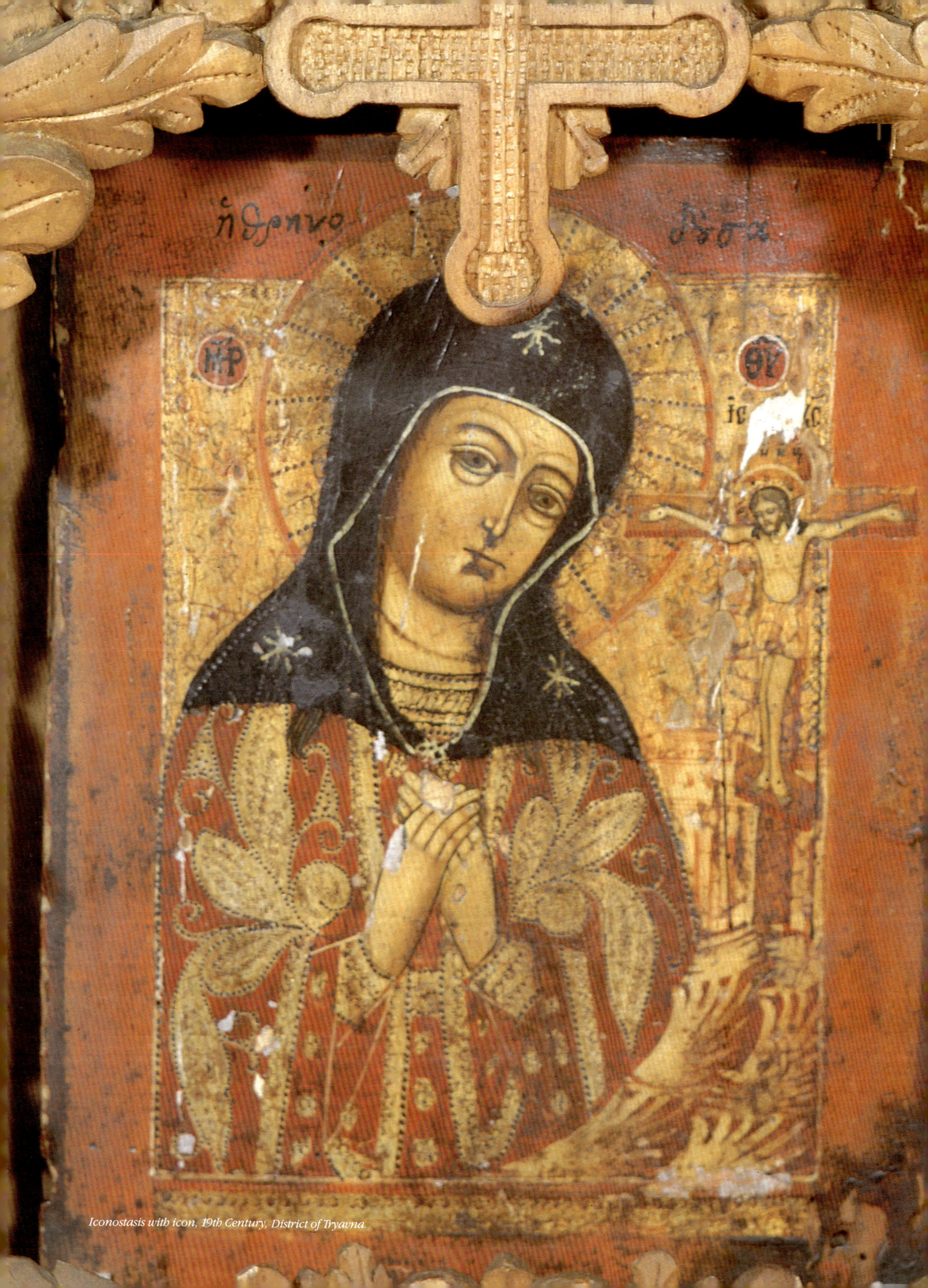

Iconostasis with icon, 19th Century, District of Tryavna.

Church Art

Vesela Vassileva

With the adoption of Christianity in Bulgaria in 865, the political organisation of the state, language and culture was paralleled by the organising role of the Church and of the Christian cult in the process of consolidation of Bulgarian nationhood. The membership of the Eastern Orthodox community was one of the features of the self-determination of the Bulgarians during the different historical epochs. This was particularly strongly manifested in the struggle for the preservation of Bulgarian nationhood during the five-centuries long Ottoman domination. Very indicative in this respect is the strong national and religious consciousness of the Bulgarians in the struggle for an independent Church during the period of the Bulgarian National Revival, which resulted in the formation of the Bulgarian Exarchate in 1870.

The worshipping as national saints of such persons, canonised by the Bulgarian Church and associated with Bulgarian history, as the brothers Cyril and Methodius who created the Slav script and literature, Prince Boris-Michail I who imposed Christianity on the Bulgarian people the famous man of letters Kliment of Ochrida, of the students and disciples of Cyril and Methodius and other outstanding personalities testifies to the national character of the cult, to the historical determination and ethnic colour of Bulgarian Church Art.

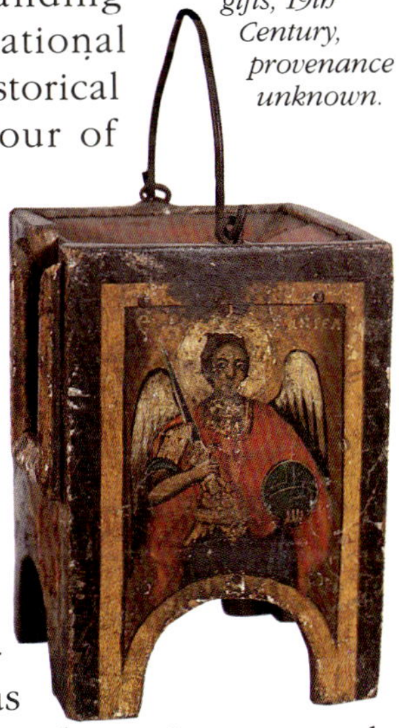

Box for keeping gifts, 19th Century, provenance unknown.

The idea of the high historical values of the Bulgarians and the greatness of their political and spiritual leaders was advocated in the years of foreign domination for the preservation of the national consciousness and the national identity, using all means at the disposal of the Church organisation and of the Christian cult, as well as the various genres of Church art, icons, mural paintings and prints in a mass circulation. This was particularly true of the period of Ottoman domination when martyrs who had perished in the struggle against the forced Islamisation and Turkisation of Bulgarians, found their place in the Bulgarian Christian Pantheon side by side with the old saints. Such new saints were the New St. George of Sofia, the New St. Nicholas of Sofia, Bishop Vissaryon of Smolyan, the New St. Dimiter, St. Zlata of Muglen, and others. During the Bulgarian National Revival period the idea of a secular celebration of the day of Cyril and Methodius was taken up and this day grew rapidly from a Church holiday to a national day of Bulgarian writing, education and culture. Being a symbol of the striving towards knowledge and spiritual upsurge, the day of Cyril and Methodius (May 24th) is one of the most treasured holidays in present-day Bulgaria.

The survey of the ways in which Christianity participated in the formation and in the historical development of Bulgarian culture would be incomplete if one failed to study the specific features of Church art that served this development and was created in the course of the history of the Bulgarian people. From the very first decades after the adoption of Christianity, Church architecture and art played an important role in the understanding of religion, for informing the people about their history and about the life of the saints.

It is particularly interesting to trace the continuity between paganism and Christianity and the projections of this continuity in the various spheres; in the cult and Church rituals, in the folk festive ritual system and in everyday life. In parallel with the inherited paganism, the Christian religion was at the basis of the so-called folk Christianity (also referred to as Orthodox Christian paganism), which was a complex combination of Christianity and paganism, of religious doctrine and folk traditions. On the one hand, the new religion gave the opportunity of a Christian interpretation of the inherited elements and preservation of the customs and beliefs corresponding to them. On the other hand, a number of pagan relicts have found a place in the Christian cult and in the Christian Pantheon.

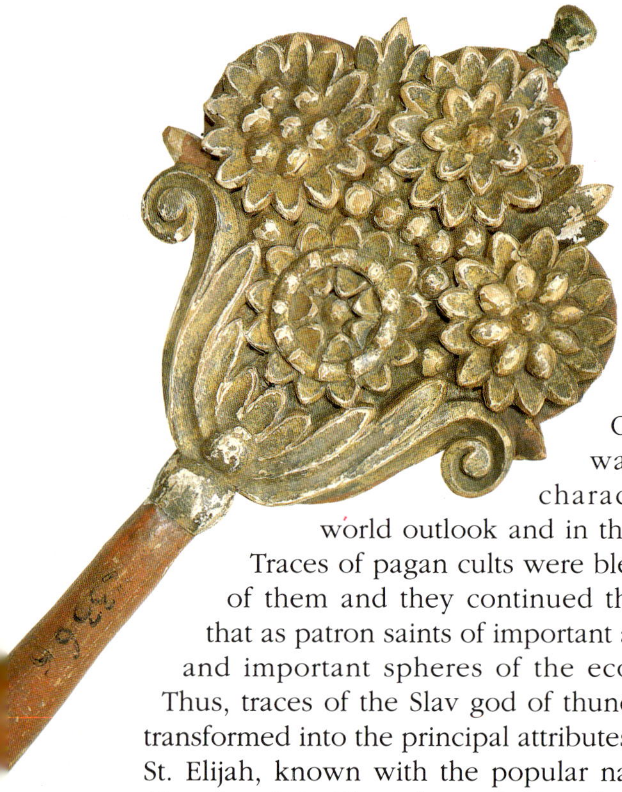

Gonfalon, 19th Century, Elena.

The folk interpretation of the Christian saints was an important characteristic in the world outlook and in the festive system. Traces of pagan cults were blended into many of them and they continued their vitality after that as patron saints of important aspects of nature and important spheres of the economic activity. Thus, traces of the Slav god of thunder, Perun, were transformed into the principal attributes and qualities of St. Elijah, known with the popular names *grumovnik* (thunderer) St. Vlas inherited some features of the god Volos and was worshipped as the patron-saint of domestic animals. The Thracian Heros together with some other pre-Christian relicts outlined the image of St. George, the dragon-fighter. Relicts of ancient cults and beliefs concerning the Great Mother - Goddess centered around the image of the Mother of God. Finally there was a correspondence between the Thracian goddess Artemis-Bendis and some elements in the cult of St. Marina, who was worshipped throughout Bulgaria as a protectress against fires, as a patron-saint of snakes and as a healer. Traces of the Dionysus cult can be detected in his successor, St. Tryphon. His iconography was influenced by folk notions and he usually appeared on icons with a pruning-knife in his hand.

The folk Christian Calendar of holidays is organised on an economic pre-Christian basis. The Christianised festive annual cycle preserved the old pagan system of time organisation, centered around the winter and summer solstice (St. Ignatius' Day, Christmas and Midsummer Day) and the equinox in spring and in autumn (the Day of the Holy Infants (Mladentsi) and St.Symeon's Day (the Day of the Elevation of the Cross).

Traces of the ancient paganism can also be detected in the folk beliefs, outlook and the social normative structure, as well as in the ritual and festive system. In its turn, this intermixing of the two principal tendencies is observed in works of art servicing the cult. Various elements of the Bulgarian's way of life are reflected in the church decoration, (the mural paintings more specifically), which are an interesting historical source about the life of the society. The portraits of the church donors betray a realism and they often depict the particular characteristics of the clothing of the people portrayed. Painted scenes from church decoration like "The Wheel of Life", "The Day of Judgement", "At the Fortune-Teller", "The Righteous" and "The Sinners" reveal interesting elements connected with the folk notions about time, about good and evil, about morality and sin.

Icons are an invariable part of Bulgarian church art. Bulgaria was the first Slav state in which icon-painting gained popularity in parallel with the spreading of Christianity in the 9th century. In its historical evolution the art of the icon was associated with the most

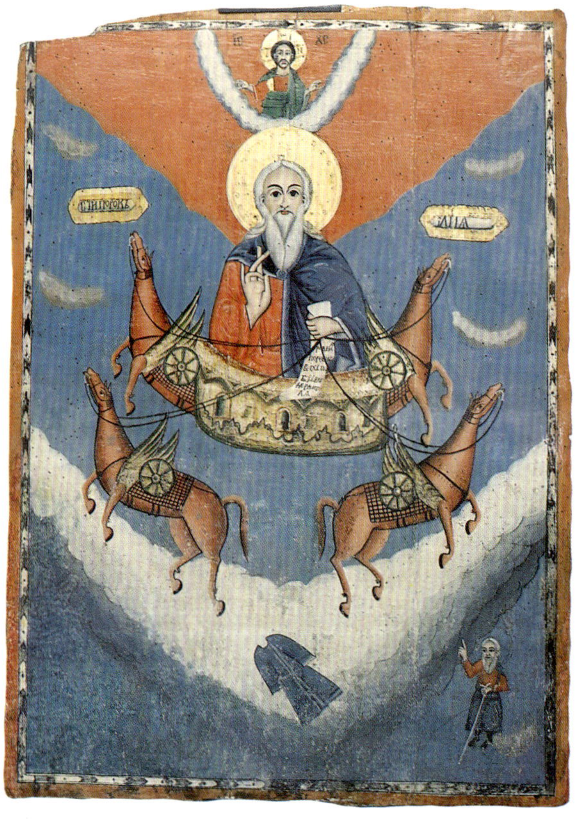

Icon of St. Elijah, 19th Century, Tryavna School, Turnovo.

Tryptych, 19th Century, Tryavna.

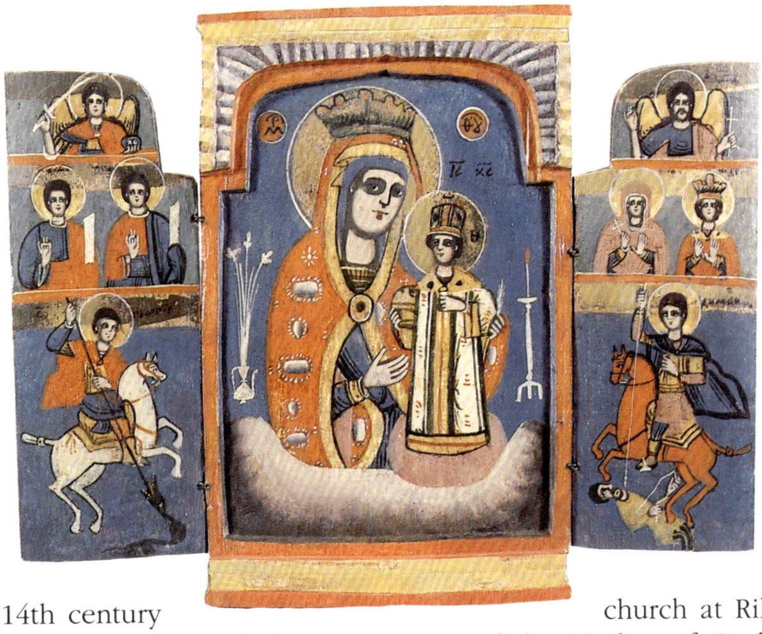

outstanding periods of Bulgarian culture, with the consolidation of its contribution to the general evolution of art and with the preservation of the Bulgarian national spirit throughout the centuries of Ottoman domination.

Bulgarian icon art experienced its greatest upsurge after the 10th century and reached its highest peaks in the 12th-14th century when Bulgaria was a leading centre from which the use of icons spread to the entire Slav world and in the Balkan Peninsula. The images of the icons enjoy the greatest emotional impact among the works of official art. A unique example of monumental art can be seen in the glazed ceramic icon of St. Theodore Stratilates (9th-10th century) from the Patleina monastery near the capital city of that time, Preslav. The stern and majestic image, executed with great professional skill, justifiably defines this work as one of the masterpieces of Balkan Christian art. The icon-painting tradition continued during the period of Byzantine domination (1018-1185). Ochrida, Sofia, Nerezi and some other places in the lands of the former Bulgarian state gave birth to remarkable monumental paintings, various icons made of wood with metal casings, enamel, and marble reliefs. There is extensive information on this in the typicon of the Bachkovo Monastery, which contains inventories of icons. During the period of the Second Bulgarian State (1186-1396), the art of icon-painting, miniature and mural painting was enriched and developed in the country's main political and cultural centre - the capital Turnovo. The large number of fragments preserved in the churches in Tsarevets and Trapezitsa, monuments like the frescoes in the Church of the Forty Holy Martyrs, in the Boyana church near Sofia, in the Zemen Monastery and elsewhere, which have survived after numerous foreign incursions, wars and disasters, are eloquent evidence of the remarkable flourishing of Church art in the 13th-19th century.

The icons of that period that have survived to our times, such as the two-sided icon of Christ Pantocrator from Nessebur, the icon of St. John of Rila from the old church at Rila Monastery, the Eleousa icon of the Mother of God, dated 1311, with silver casing, (found in the church of Bachkovo Monastery) represent only a small part of the best works of the Bulgarian icon-painting tradition. Together they give an idea about the severe, laconic and majestic style, the classical proportions, the exquisite line and colours which characterize the official art of the Bulgarians.

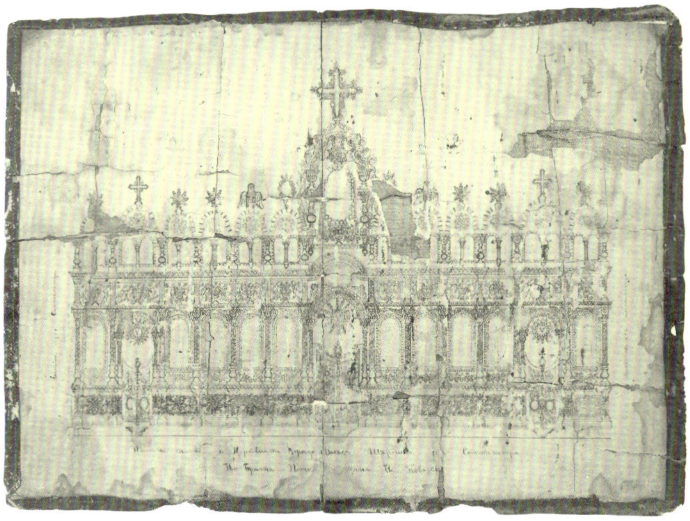

Plan for iconostasis.

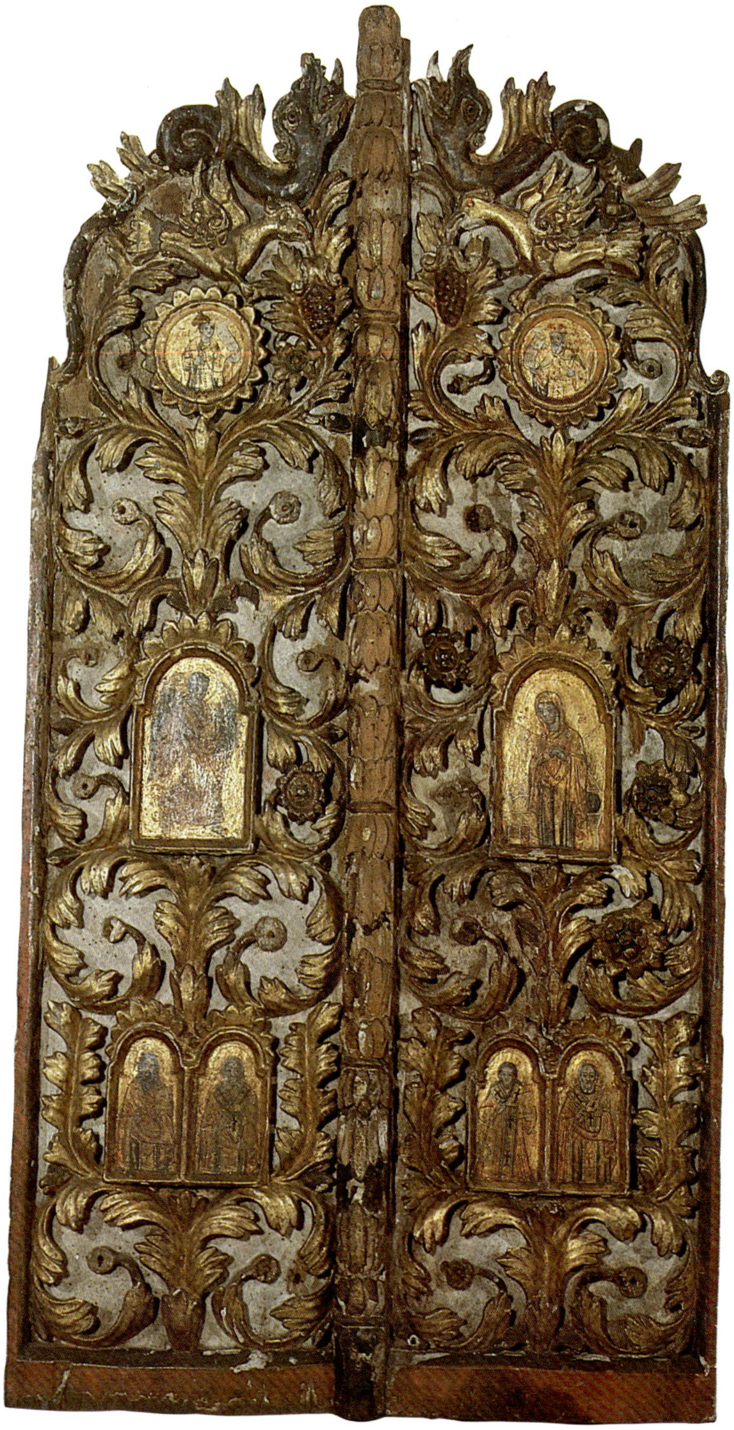

Altar gates for Iconostasis, 19th Century, Zlatitsa.

The upsurge in the socio-economic, political and cultural life during the period of the Bulgarian National Revival at the end of the 18th and in the early 19th century resulted in the development of several art schools - in Tryavna, Samokov and Bansko - from which dozens of icon-painters and thousands of icons were born. A new stylistic outlook and a new ideal of beauty became apparent in the works of the icon-painters. The works of such famous artists as Simeon Tsanyov, Tsanyu Zahariev, Dimiter Kunchov and others from the Tryavna school adorn churches and monasteries all over the country and even abroad. The Tryavna Art School transcended the boundaries of a local phenomenon in its significance.

Artists from Samokov, notably Dimiter Zograph, Zahari Zograph, Ivan Obrazopisov, Nikola Obrazopisov and Stanislav Dospevski painted many icons which can be found now in the Rila, Bachkovo, Troyan, Preobrazhenski monasteries, in Smokov, Koprivshtitsa and Mount Athos, which stand out with their markedly national style, noble colours and elegance. The artistic style of Toma Vishanov, Dimiter Molerov and Simeon Molerov from Bansko betrays the strong influence of Western art.

An integral part of the interior decoration of churches during the period of the Bulgarian National Revival became the high iconostasis wall for which many bigger and smaller icons were painted, while the wood-carved iconostasis became the centre of the plastic decoration.

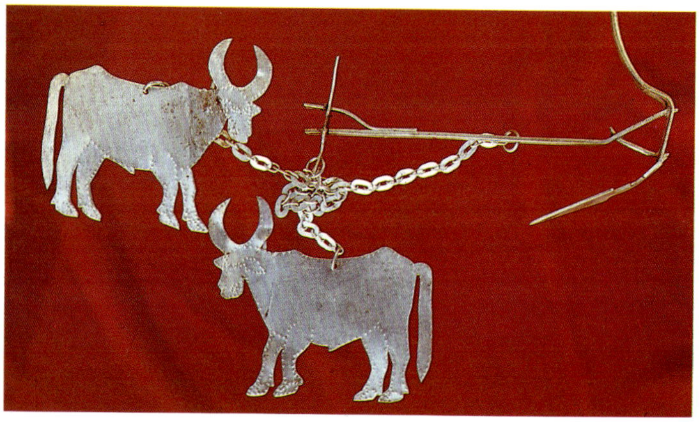

Votive, oxen with plough, 19th Century, Provenance unknown.

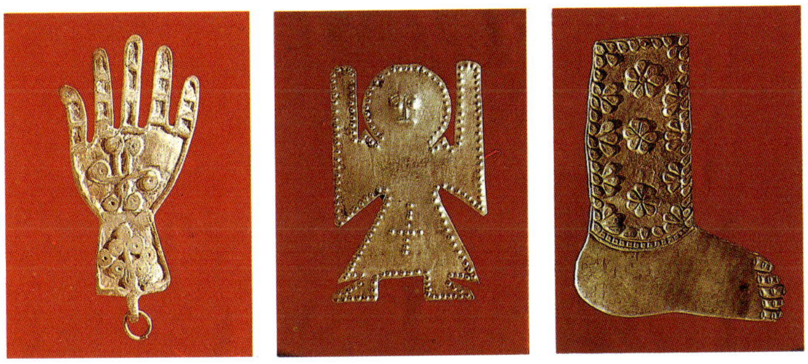

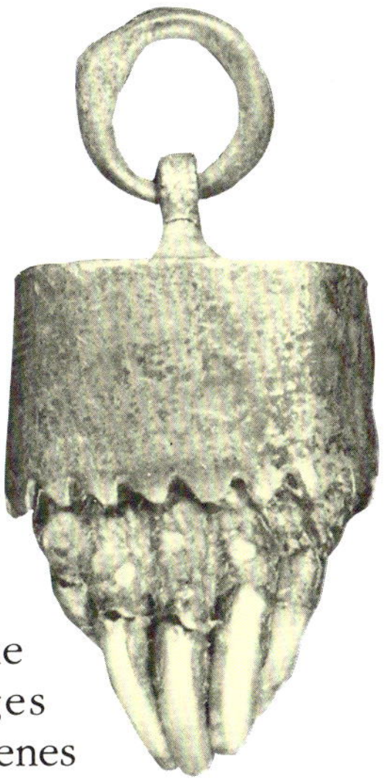

Amulet, tortoise foot in cast silver, 19th Century, Provenance unknown.

Bulgarian church woodcarving, which remotely echoed the 9th century Byzantine tradition, displayed great variety in overcoming the strict canonic requirement of the Church. The artists/woodcarvers manifested quite substantial freedom in the choice of motifs, symbols and images. Bulgarian church woodcarving evolved as a result of a peculiar cultural-historical and artistic development. It was a synthesis of religious content, folk beliefs and notions, national-liberation symbols, impressions from the surrounding reality and reinterpreted influences of various artistic styles.

Throughout its centuries-long evolution, the art of church wood carving has been enriched and yet has preserved its characteristic Bulgarian style. Several art centres flourished during the period of the Bulgarian National Revival, notably the woodcarving schools in Debar, Bansko, Samokov and Tryavna, which developed their own characteristic stylistic features. The highly professional masterpieces of iconostases, for example in the church of the Holy Mother of God in Pazardjik, the old chapel in the cemetery of Bansko, the iconostasis of the Church in the Rila Monastery and dozens of others, came from the hand of Bulgarian woodcarvers to become a part of the treasurehouse of Bulgarian folk culture.

The present Exhibition includes a collection of votive plates and amulets. According to the folk beliefs of the Bulgarians, in cases of illness in the family, misfortune, poor harvest, or death of the domestic animals, they were offered in the form of *obrok* (votive tablet) to a church or to a monastery, praying for the help and protection of a certain saint. According to their purpose, these votive tablets can contain a motif of gratitude or a motif of good wishes. Usually these *obroks* are the work of local goldsmiths, they are in the form of figures made of metal (silver alloy), with wrought decoration, which are suspended from the icons.

Various types of amulets were used for protection against the evil forces, according to the folk beliefs of the Bulgarians from the late 19th and early 20th century. The actual amulets were objects made of metal, wood, and bone often decorated with symbolic images typical of Christianity such as biblical scenes and symbols. Ordinary objects to which apotropaic properties were ascribed were also used; flowers, teeth and tusks, animal horns, coins and necklaces.

Church art with its architectural and cultural monuments forms a part of the cultural and historical heritage of the Bulgarian nation. The People's Republic of Bulgaria is making great efforts to protect, preserve, restore and reconstruct sites of historical importance, irrespective of the religious denomination with which they are associated. Churches, monasteries, mosques, architectural and cult complexes are covered by the programmes for protection of the cultural and historical heritage of the Bulgarian nation. They are important evidence for studying the eventful and even tempestuous history of the Bulgarian lands and for the preservation of the ethnic and cultural unity and traditions of the Bulgarians.

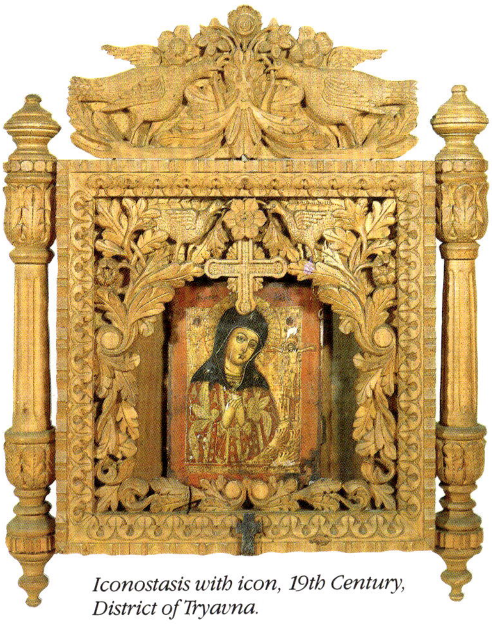

Iconostasis with icon, 19th Century, District of Tryavna.

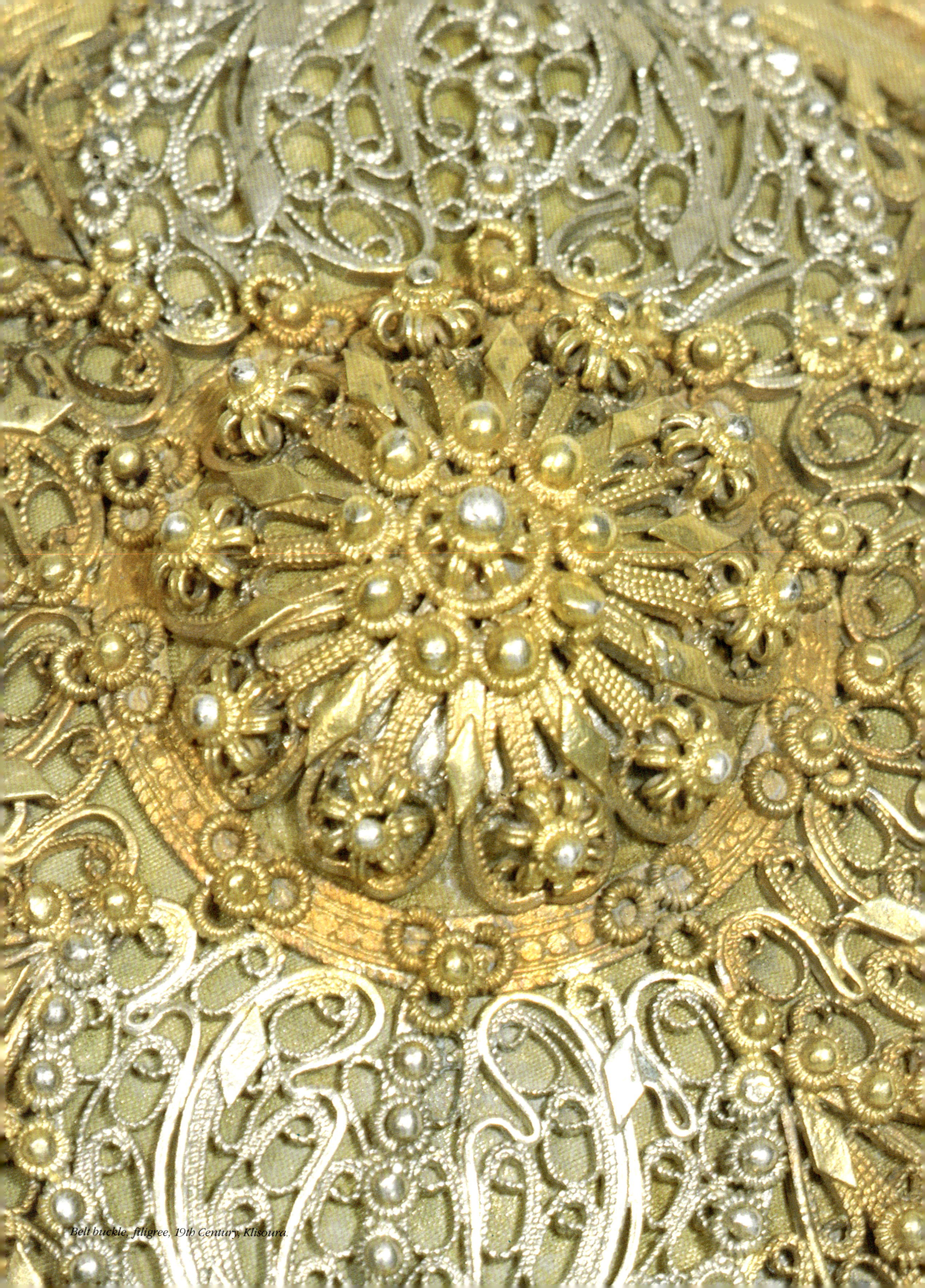

Belt buckle, filigree, 19th Century, Klisoura.

Jewellery and Adornment

Snezhana Blagoeva

With their origins in the ancient culture Bulgarian traditional decorations bear the signs of the same mythological concepts and superstitions which created such beings as Rada and the dragon's sweetheart. Throughout this centuries-old development are combined the primitive function of the metal decoration, ancient war-tribal and ruler's insignia signs and symbols of folk culture and, last but not least, the skill of the Bulgarian goldsmiths.

The peculiar significance of gold is well known in the mythological beliefs of humankind. It was a common belief among many peoples that this metal could pass unhindered over the boundaries between worlds and play the role of cosmic mediator. Due to the same superstitious belief the golden hue was common to gods, the dead and the initiated. The concept of gold-fire-sun were interchangeable. Traits of these archaic beliefs have been preserved to the present day in traditional Bulgarian culture.

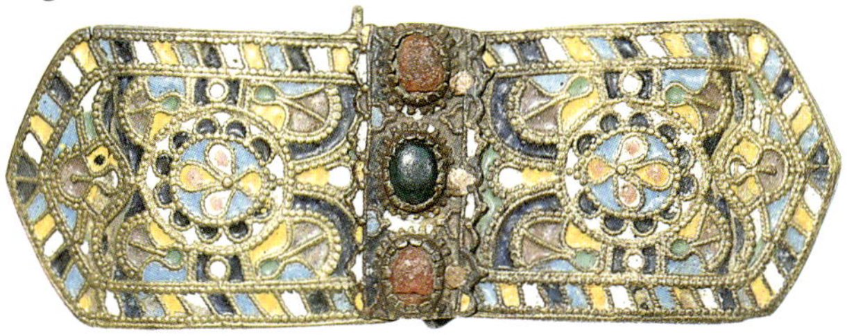

Enamelled belt buckle, 18th – 19th Century, West Bulgaria.

In folk mythology and in the ritual practices of the Bulgarians the key symbols of gold and silver are almost identical. According to some beliefs these metals possess marked magically-protective qualities, possibly based on empirical knowledge of the now scientifically proved anti-bacterial properties of precious metals. In Bulgarian culture the Slavonic name of this metal was used for naming the craftsmen who, in fact, used to make decorations not only of gold, but also of silver, non-ferrous metals and alloys. According to folk superstition, the high mythological and semiotical properties of gold are reflected in its application to traditional decoration. The same applies to the use of silver.

The socio-economical and cultural differences of old societies have left their mark on the design of Bulgarian personal adornment. In their development is reflected the social stratification and polarisation of culture in class societies. This differentiation is clearly reflected in the use of precious and non-precious non-ferrous metals in adornments made of silver alloys and bronze with gold being reserved mainly for plating and coin decoration.

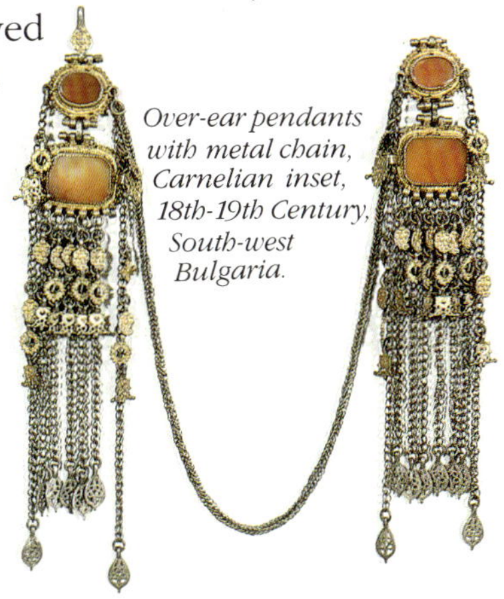

Over-ear pendants with metal chain, Carnelian inset, 18th-19th Century, South-west Bulgaria.

The design of the Bulgarian folk decorations has been influenced by the succession of cultures inhabiting the Bulgarian lands: the typical style and technical skill of Thracian metal sculpture, Roman and Byzantine decorative elements, the form of the Slavonic 'over-the-ear' pendants and motifs from ProtoBulgarian belt decoration. The use of these motifs in recent times is proof of the vitality of artistic tradition in the Bulgarian goldsmith's craft during the five centuries of Ottoman rule when Bulgarian folk decorations were influenced by Oriental style.

The type and local-regional variety in the development of the traditional metal decorative wear is clearly marked in the period of Bulgarian National Revival

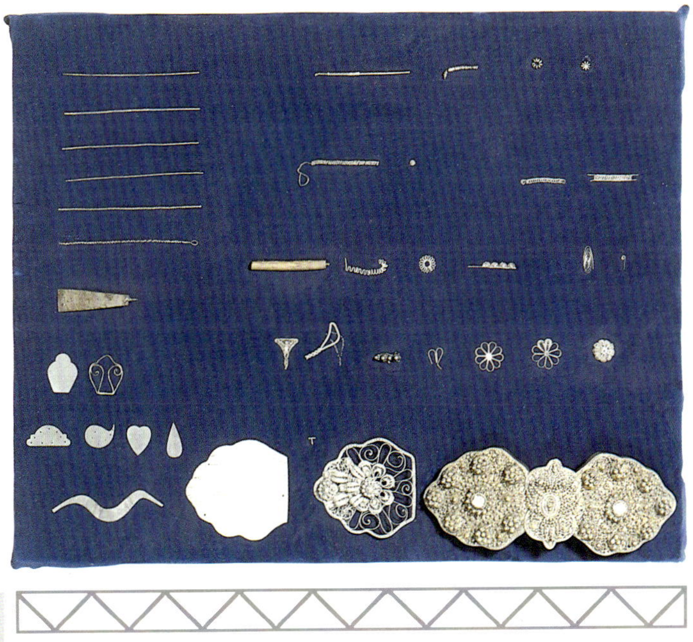

Filigree technique.

(18th to 19th century) when distinct goldsmith's centres came into being and were developed as specific folk-art schools. The centuries-old tradition in the processing of precious and non-precious non-ferrous metals and the social homogeneity of the Bulgarian society in the years of Ottoman oppression define the characteristic folk design of decorations both in their ethnic and social aspects.

The decorations of this period were made with the local variants of the ancient and traditional jeweller's techniques: forging and hammering images in relief, casting, filigree and enamelling.

The master goldsmiths of the Revival gradually abandoned the geometrical and schematic style of the ornamentation of the Middle Ages. The ideographic principle gradually loses ground and the geometrical pattern-signs and symbols are gradually replaced by the naturalistically treated motifs. The forms and the design of folk decorations of the Revival period are a continuation of the ancient traditions in the artistic interpretation of palmations and rosettes. This is also the period which experienced an influx of new ideas, taken from West-European neo-classical styles (renaissance, baroque and rococo) which are adopted and given a new functional interpretation. Eastern influences can be found in some new forms and designs, for example compositions of poplars, strawberries and roses. The influence of designs from wall-paintings and wood-carving also affects the design of jewellery. Alongside the foreign influences the Bulgarian master goldsmiths copied surrounding nature: flowering hollyhocks and tulips, leaves and stalks from the Bulgarian gardens, skilfully interlaced with the foreign ornamental motifs.

In the period of the Revival decorations for the traditional costume proved to be more conservative compared with the decorations for the new urban dress for which many of the showy but heavy and impractical head and bosom decorations were gradually abandoned. It is characteristic of this period that the head decorations of most of the traditional costumes still bear traditional elements and continue to display regional differences.

The 'over-the-ear' pendants and ear-rings are typically Slavonic. They are the accepted decoration for all bridal head-dresses of recent times, but ear-rings have also been worn by maidens and sometimes (as required by some superstitious beliefs) even by men. Eastern influences are very strong in the design of the temporal bone pendant called a "claw". Together with the small

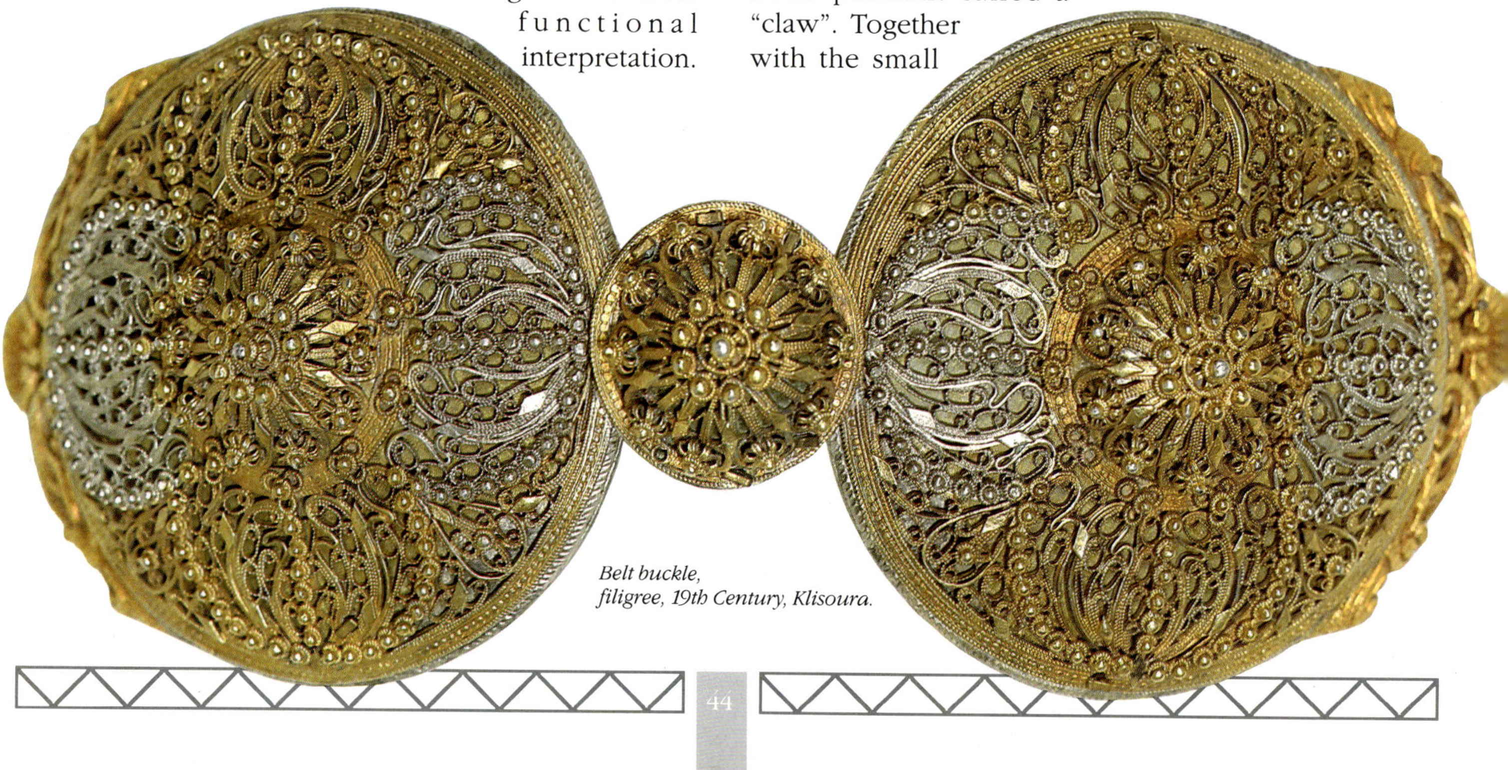

Belt buckle, filigree, 19th Century, Klisoura.

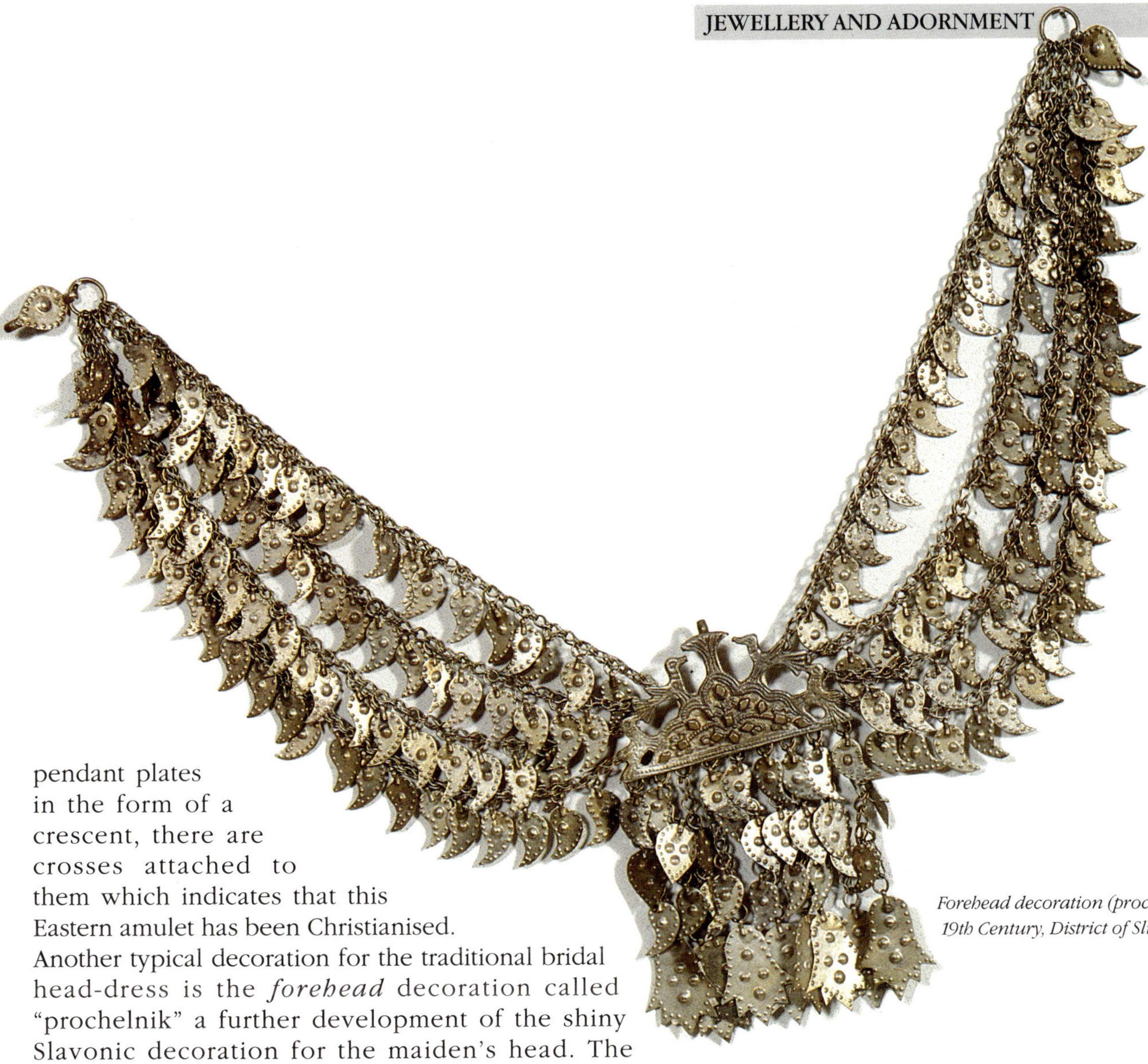

Forehead decoration (prochelnik), 19th Century, District of Sliven.

pendant plates in the form of a crescent, there are crosses attached to them which indicates that this Eastern amulet has been Christianised.
Another typical decoration for the traditional bridal head-dress is the *forehead* decoration called "prochelnik" a further development of the shiny Slavonic decoration for the maiden's head. The ribbons with metal plates sewn to them, known in the Middle Ages, are a continuation of this tradition, well-preserved in the epoch of Ottoman rule. The forehead decorations made during that period are of various designs in the different regions but they are all laid on the bridal head-dress in circular form, which, according to some superstitious beliefs, is a sign of protection against evil forces. The existence of interlaced vegetal elements and birds is not purely decorative. In scientific research they are considered to be a semantic variant of the tree of life, bearing great marital symbolism.
The hair-pins are also of various regional forms and serve for fixing up the kerchief. Perhaps under Oriental influence they developed into another type of decoration, the "trepki", having a number of pendant chains with decorative plates. According to superstitious beliefs the sound they made drove away evil forces and the evil eye.
The decoration for the crown of the head "tepeluk" is another bridal decoration in the form of a round plate either curved or flat. Its vegetal ornaments are of Eastern and West-European decorative elements but usually the crown decorations are designed as Christian amulets with images of iconographic subject-matters such as "The Miracle of St. George and the Dragon".
St. George is a very popular subject in Bulgarian art. According to folk beliefs he is a protector of love and marriage and perhaps this symbolic meaning is reflected in the use of his image on the Bulgarian head decorations. *The under-the-chin decorative chain, called "podbradnik"*, serves to attach the elaborately styled bridal head-dress to the head. It is sometimes attached to the over-the-ear pendants forming a matching adornment. *The metal pendants "Kosichnitsi"* are hung on the back of the hair. Some of them are a sophisticated decorative composition with long pendant chains.
Though modified to a certain extent, separate patterns of breast decoration found throughout the Bulgarian lands in ancient times and the Middle Ages continued to exist even up to and including the period of Revival.

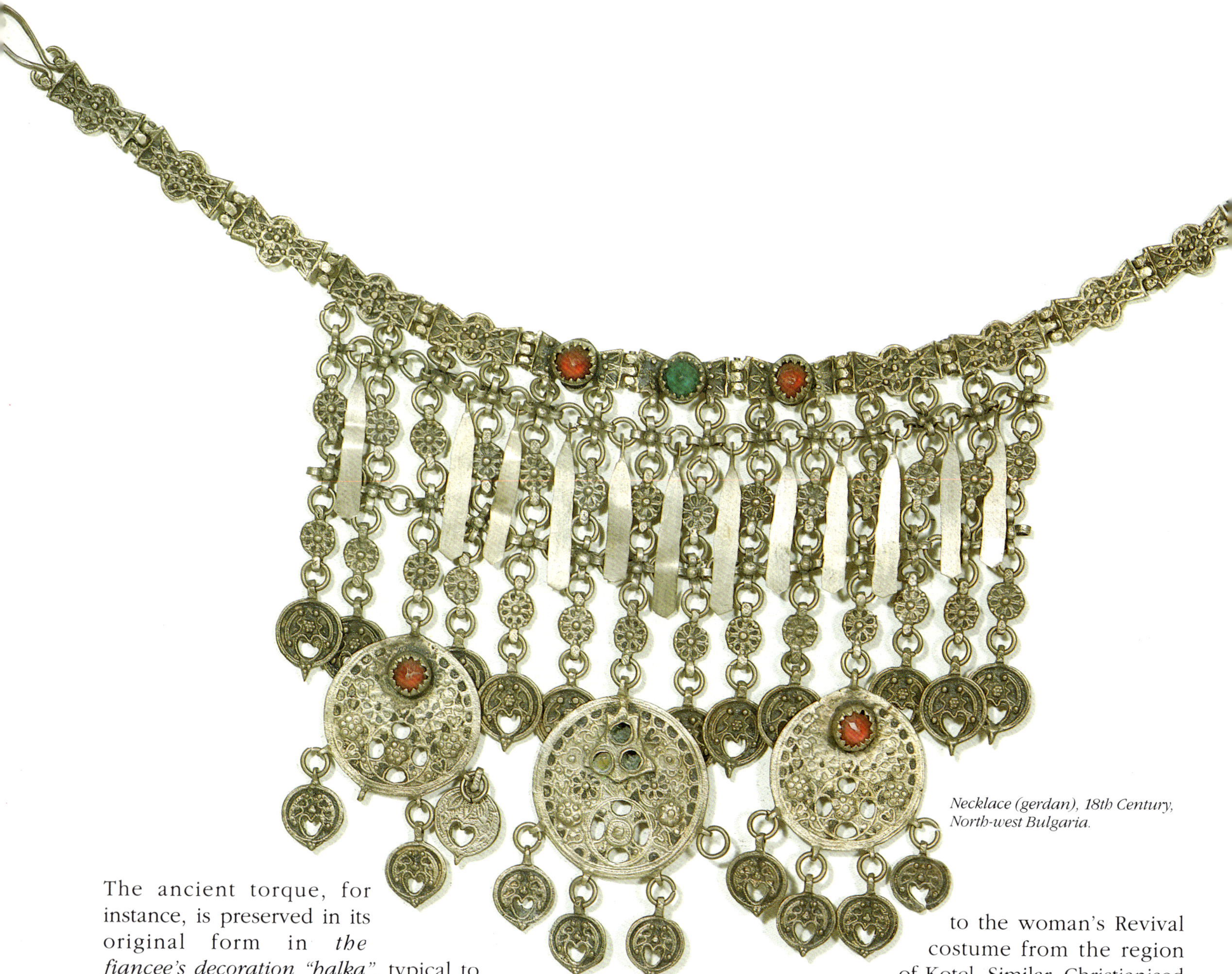

Necklace (gerdan), 18th Century, North-west Bulgaria.

The ancient torque, for instance, is preserved in its original form in *the fiancee's decoration "halka"*, typical to the region of Kotel. In the 18th century and the beginning of the 19th century a typical decoration was *the necklace, known under the Eastern name "gerdan"*. It bears a distant affiliation with the Bulgarian aristocratic decorations of the Middle Ages, luxuriously decorated with enamel. The later patterns are their simpler cast variants. Among the variety of traditional necklaces two main types are conspicuous: those close-fitting to the neck and the longer ones falling over the breast. Almost all of them have pendants which are different in form and length. The breast decoration "kouna" (icon) is typical to the woman's Revival costume from the region of Kotel. Similar, Christianised amulet-icons are known in other regions of the country. They are found in the shape of a round, triangular or quadrangular box-reliquary with embossed iconographic images, personages and twin-headed eagles, often interlaced with pagan symbols.

The buttons used in the clothing of the Middle Ages continued to be used in later times but became flatter and had hooks for fastening. *A typical decoration is the "kitka"* in South-West Bulgaria which serves to join up with two ends of the bosom of the woman's chemise by means of hooks which are very similar to the ancient fibulae.

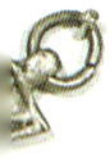

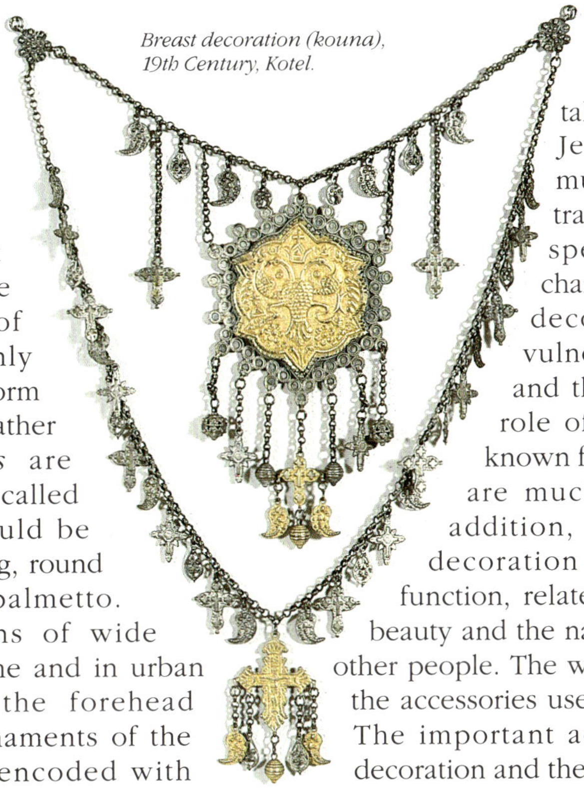

Breast decoration (kouna), 19th Century, Kotel.

To the category of body decorations *belong the metal belts.* In the Middle Ages these were worn predominantly by men. This tradition was kept alive until later times in some regions but in the period of Ottoman rule they were mainly used by women. They take the form of decorative chips stuck on leather or fabric. *The belt buckles* are artistically-made metal plates, called "pafti". Their rich variety could be classified in three groups: oblong, round and in the shape of Indian palmetto. These are bridal decorations of wide application in both folk costume and in urban Revival clothing. As with the forehead decoration, the decorative ornaments of the bridal belt and buckles are encoded with ancient symbols and signs of marital symbolism. *Bracelets* are usually worn one on each arm. They are overt and closed. Particularly noticeable are the massive overt bracelets called "Koubelii" because of the two raised semi-spheres on their surface. Their shape and decoration are a continuation of old mediaeval tradition in metal sculpture. The closed bracelets consist of two more parts but some are made of knitted wire.

Rings are worn by both men and women. The rings with carved images and the mediaeval rings with a round plate developed into the *"stovolati" (chairshaped) rings.* And of highly original shape is the ring known as the *"claw"*, a design taken from archery.

Jewellery and metalwork are multifunctional like other parts of traditional Bulgarian costume. Their specific feature is their symbolic character. It must be remembered that decorations are put on the most vulnerable parts of the human body and that they have always fulfilled the role of a social regulator. It is a well-known fact that maiden's metal decorations are much plainer than the bride's. In addition, since ancient times, the metal decoration has had a definitely aesthetic function, related to the natural human sense of beauty and the natural desire of man to be liked by other people. The woman's metal decoration is among the accessories used for drawing the man's attention. The important aesthetic function of traditional decoration and the new trends in the ancient tradition of metal-processing during the Revival are considered two of the main reasons for the exceptionally high achievements in the design of folk decorations of that period which have been preserved as a national heritage of high aesthetic value.

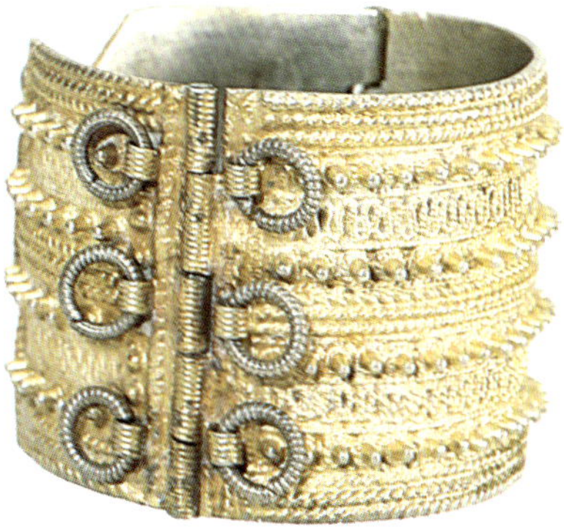

Bracelet, 18th – 19th Century, Teteven.

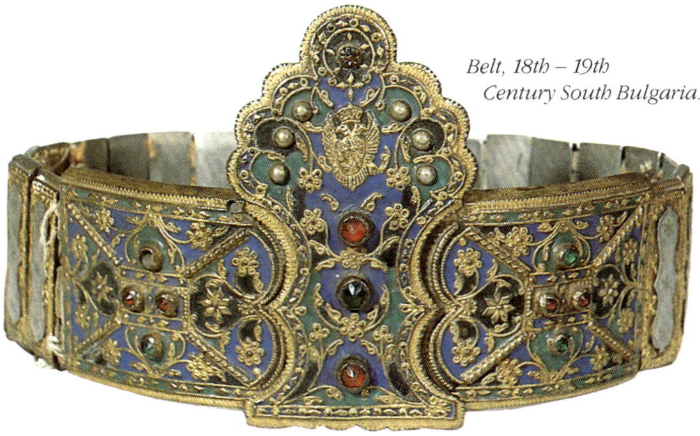

Belt, 18th – 19th Century South Bulgaria.

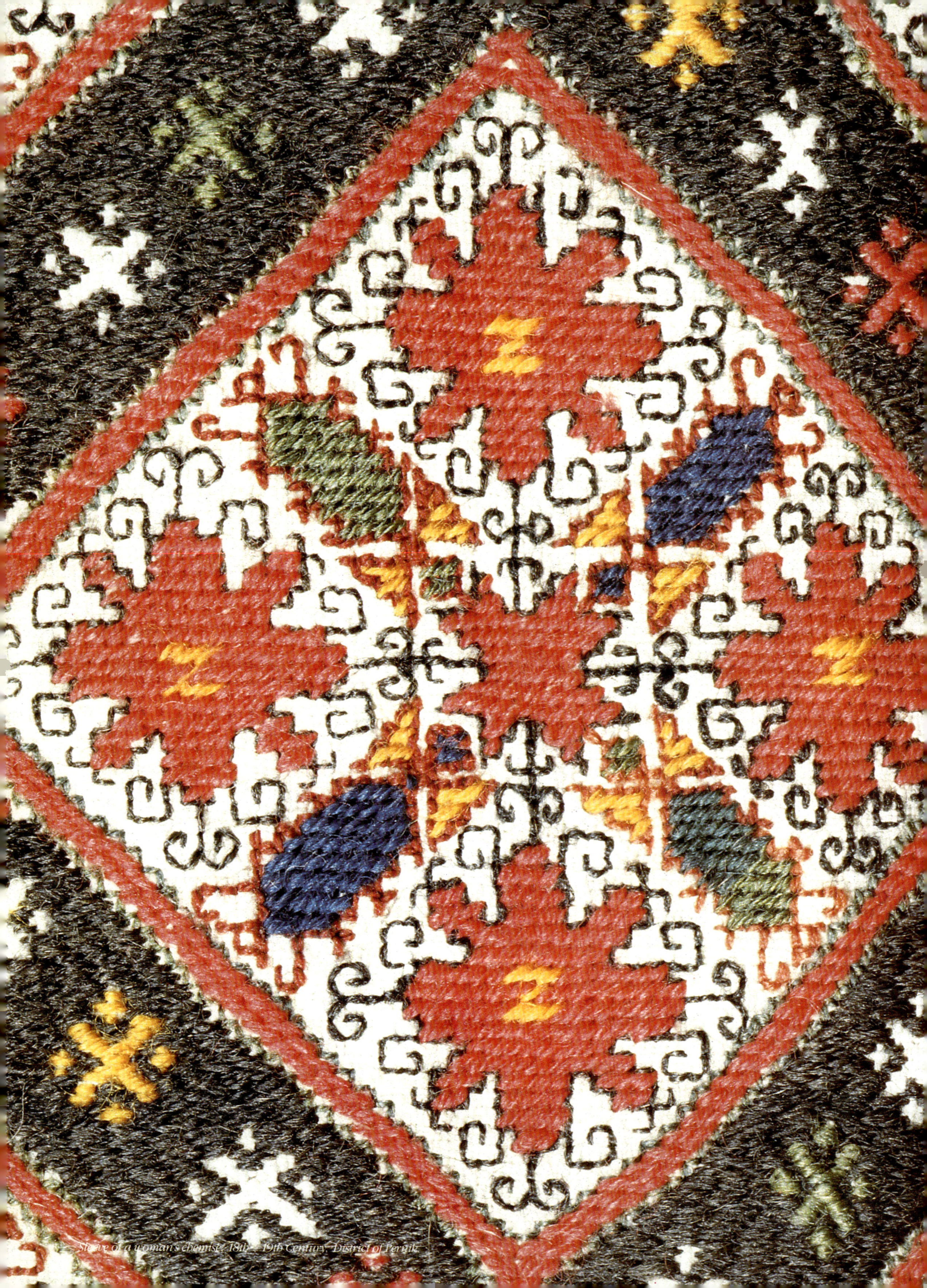

Sleeve of a woman's chemise, 18th – 19th Century, District of Pernik

Embroidery

Vesela Vassileva

".....On her skirts small stars,
On her breast the bright sun,
On her shoulders the bright moon,
On her bosom the earth and sky,
Earth, sky, forest, water,
Three mountains and a grey flock....."

Bulgarian folk embroideries are a rich fruit of the Bulgarian tradition. They are striking in their detail, richness of pattern, and numerous colour combinations. Created by Bulgarian women, the art of folk embroidery has been handed down through many generations. It is an incarnation of a profound spiritual make-up, and the aesthetic perceptions and skill of ordinary people.

Embroidery maintains the traditions of an ancient culture. Elements from this heritage are reflected not only in the structure of embroidery, its composition, pattern, colours, technique and material but also in regard to its function.

According to written records left by classical writers the Thracian women were famous for their skills in weaving and decorating fabrics made of flax and hemp. Especially skillful were the women of the Phrygian tribe who were complete masters of embroidery and ornamentation. The costumes worn in North and North-West Bulgaria have linear embroidery on the top garments, of a design considered to be Thracian in origin.

A testimony to the Slavonic base of the Bulgarian folk embroidery is its application to garments of proven Slavonic character namely, the two-garment and the "soukman" costume and the men's white-garments. The ancient embroidery with "split stitch", typical for North-West Bulgaria and some regions of South-West and South-East Bulgaria (districts of Vidin, Koula, Groudovo) is a widely distributed Slavonic feature.

Of Proto-Bulgarian origin are the head bands with rich woven ornamentation (districts of Varna, Karnobat, Kotel), the head-dresses "sokai" and "oubrous" (districts of V. Turnovo, Gabrovo, Lovech, the South-West regions) the embroidery ornamentation of the chemise "kapanka" (district of Razgrad), the cross-shaped bosom and the ornaments on sleeves from the districts of Sofia, Radomir and Trun. Close scrutiny reveals a striking similarity between Bulgarian folk embroidery ornamentation and that of the nations who were inter-related with, or enjoyed friendly relations with the Proto-Bulgarians during their passage through to the Balkans.

Limited archaeological evidence gives some information as to the character and specific features of the embroidery of the aristocratic clothing of the Middle Ages. A number of mural paintings in churches and monasteries add to our appreciation of the art of embroidery in this period. During the 15th, 16th and 17th centuries the embroidery of the Bulgarian folk costumes is noted and elaborately described in the

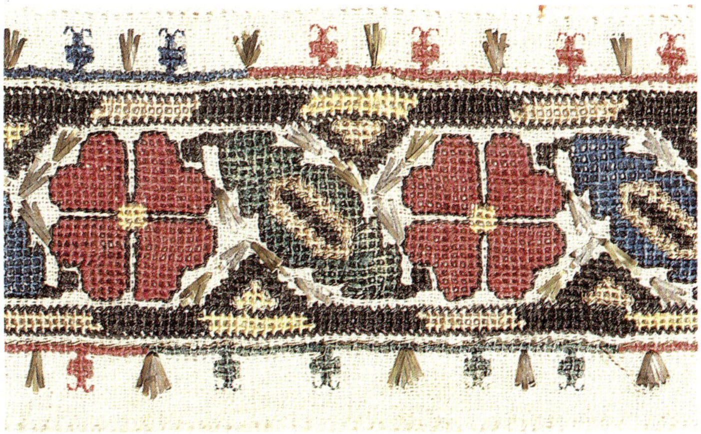

Embroidery from a headdress (sokai), 19th Century, District of Tryavna.

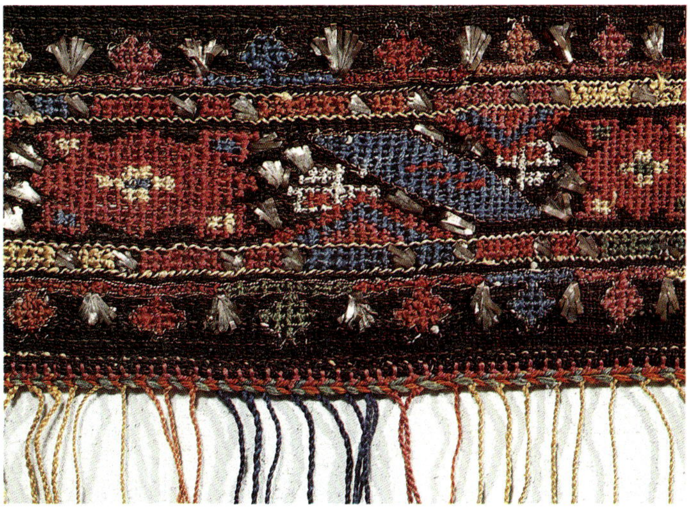

Embroidery from a headdress (sokai), 19th Century, District of Gabrovo.

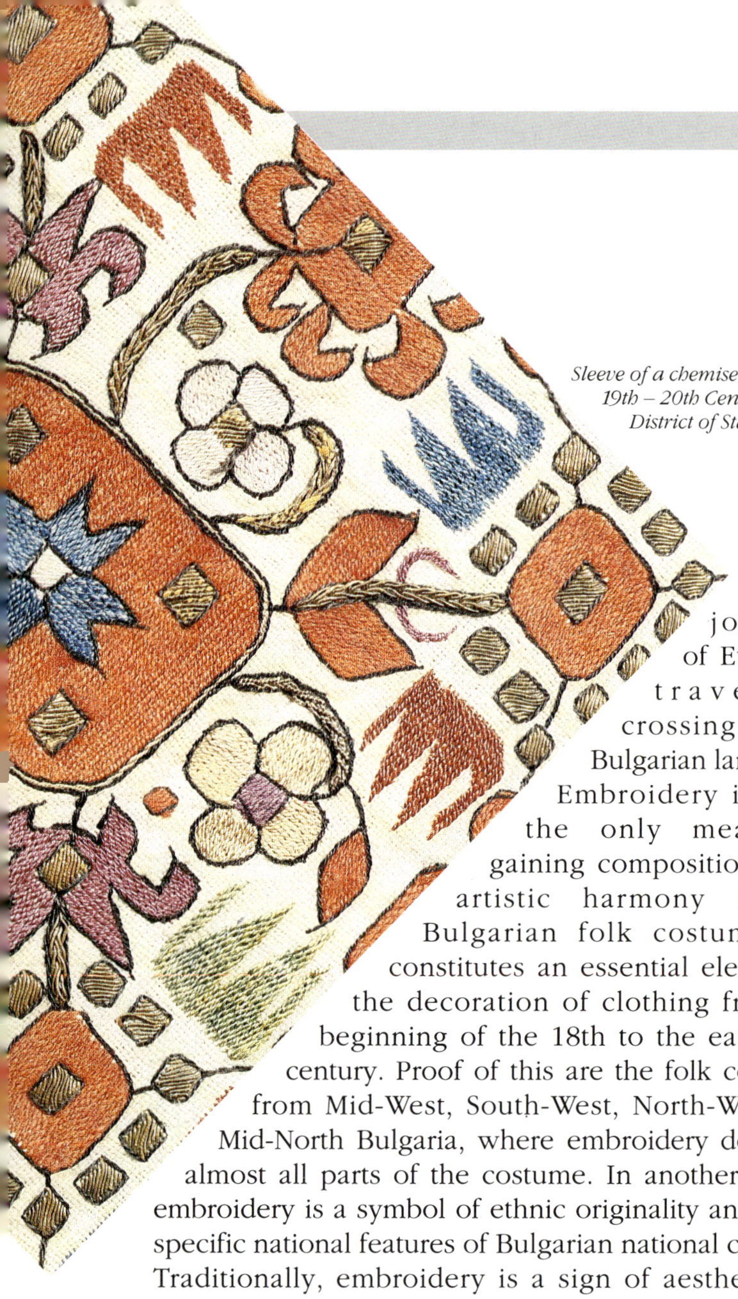

Sleeve of a chemise,
19th – 20th Century,
District of Stanke Dimitrov.

journals of European travellers crossing the Bulgarian lands.

Embroidery is often the only means of gaining compositional and artistic harmony in the Bulgarian folk costume and constitutes an essential element in the decoration of clothing from the beginning of the 18th to the early 20th century. Proof of this are the folk costumes from Mid-West, South-West, North-West and Mid-North Bulgaria, where embroidery decorates almost all parts of the costume. In another aspect, embroidery is a symbol of ethnic originality and of the specific national features of Bulgarian national costume. Traditionally, embroidery is a sign of aesthetic and religious ideas, of marital and economic status, of the aesthetic, ethnographic, regional and locational status of the people wearing it. There are, however, some regional differences and peculiarities of style. Widely known and highly esteemed are the pieces of embroidery from the districts of Sofia, Samokov, Stanke Dimitrov, Sandanski, Kjustendil, Vidin, Vratsa, Pleven, Lovech, Rousse, Razgrad, Provadia, Malko Turnovo and a number of other regions where the art of embroidery flourished until the period of National Revival when the traditional folk costume was gradually replaced by the Revival costume and urban clothing. Later on it was totally abandoned with the influx and adaptation of European fashion.

Together with its regional and ethnographic peculiarities, traditional folk embroidery proves to be a cultural indicator if great importance registered through the essential indices of material, technique, colour, ornamentation, composition and function.

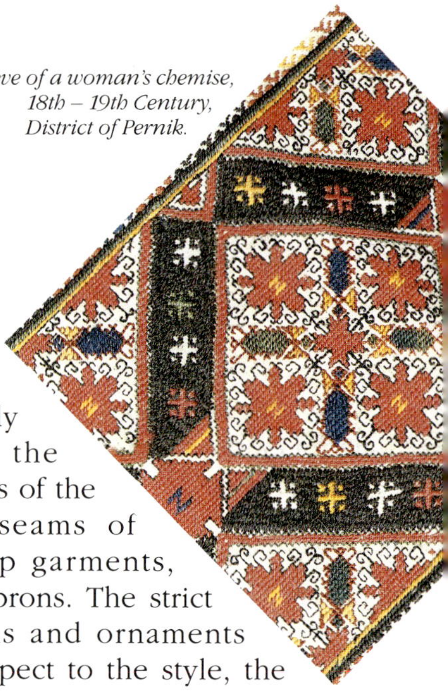

Sleeve of a woman's chemise,
18th – 19th Century,
District of Pernik.

A combination of folk aesthetics and tradition required embroidery to be used typically along the hems of the sleeves, bosoms and tails of the chemise; along the seams of underwear and on top garments, kerchiefs, towels and aprons. The strict proportions of patterns and ornaments were accorded with respect to the style, the size and function of the garment.

Bulgarian folk embroidery is worked in two ways: first embroidering by the number of the fibres of textile and secondly by embroidering a picture previously drawn on to the material in outline. The implements used by the women are a needle and thread, and in

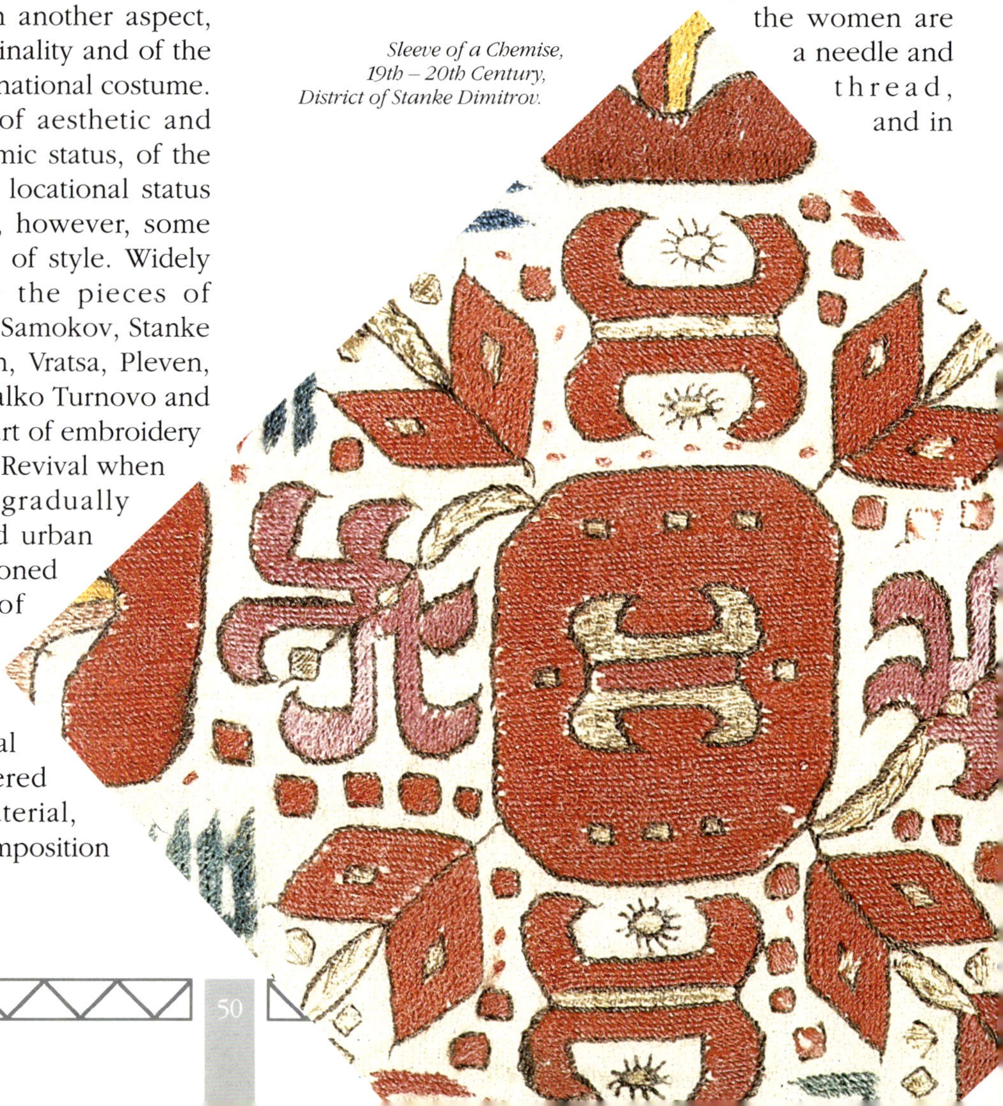

Sleeve of a Chemise,
19th – 20th Century,
District of Stanke Dimitrov.

Hem of a chemise,
19th – 20th Century, Samokov.

some regions an embroidery frame is used on which the material is stretched tight for embroidering.
The ornamentation of Bulgarian embroidery is very rich. It is a wealth of linear, geometrical, vegetal, zoomorphic and anthropomorphic figures and symbols. The exceptional variety of ornaments is a result of collective and personal experience, handed down through generations, reflecting the masters' imagination and skill.
The semantics of folk ornaments form a wide spectrum, aiming at securing health, prosperity, fertility and victory over the evil powers. In other words, it has a magic quality. Preserved by tradition, Bulgarian folk embroidery designs are a reflection of archaic mythopoetical and religious concepts.
The skill of embroidering colours has been developed to perfection. Colours and their combinations are the highly emotive part of embroidery, knitting textiles and the decoration of folk costumes. As a whole the colour range of embroidery is warm, with red the predominant tone. The harmony of colours is achieved by contrast, alternation and complementation with other colours - blue, green, yellow, white, black, brown and tinsel. With its variety, originality, beauty and exquisite style, Bulgarian folk embroidery is a reflection of profound spiritual make-up and high aesthetic criteria.

Hem of a chemise, 19th Century, District of Pernik.

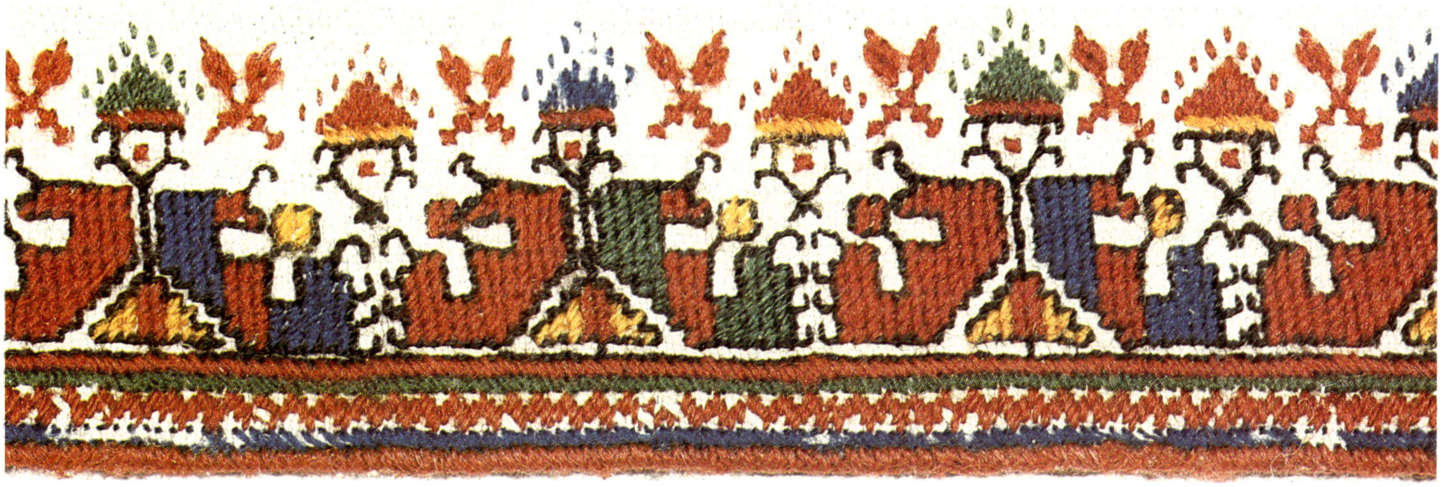

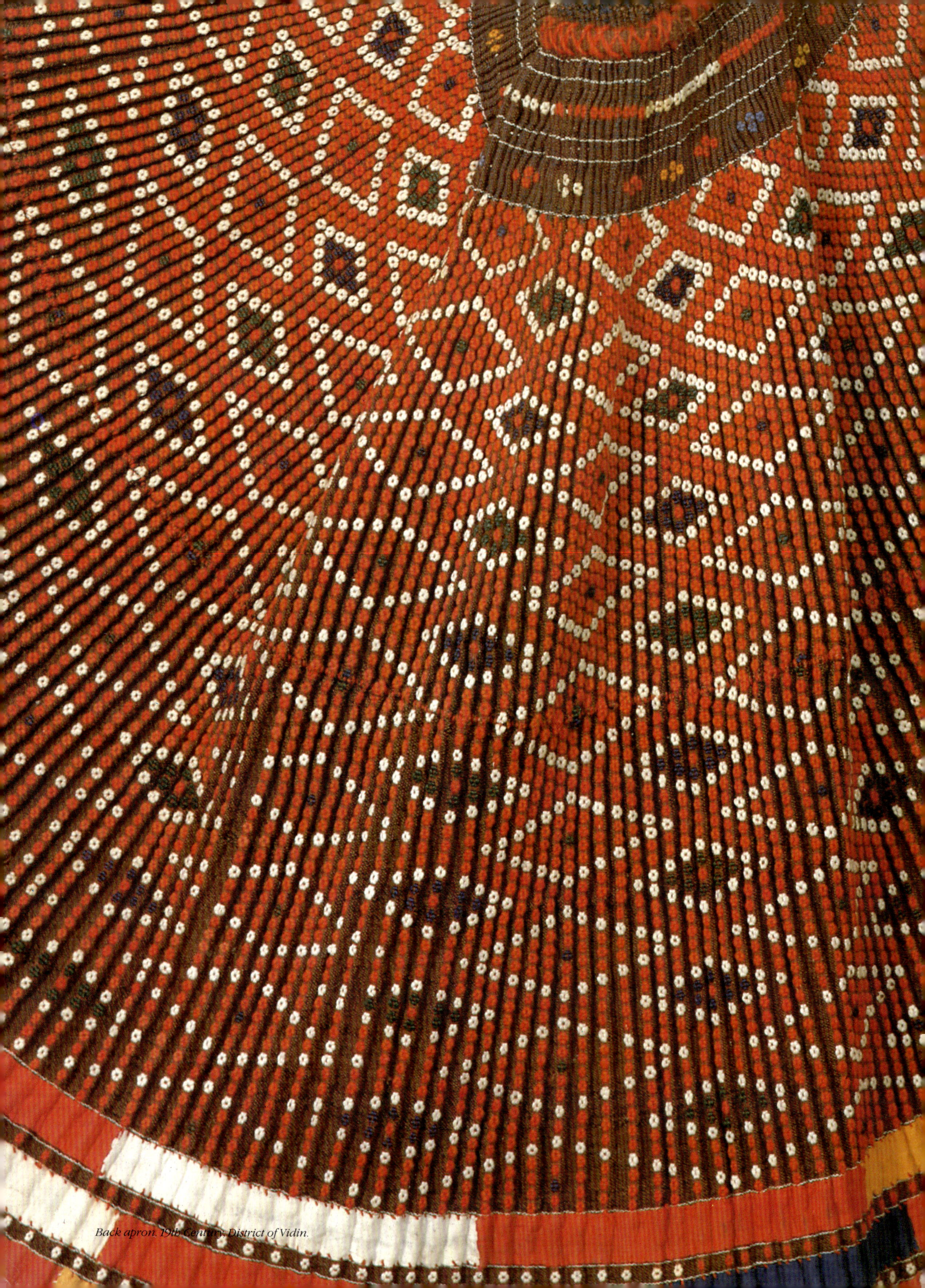

Back apron. 19th Century. District of Vidin.

Bulgarian National Costume

Marina Cherkezova

Traditional national costumes occupy an important place in the culture of the Bulgarian people. They are part of our material environment and are invariably present in the different aspects of the life of the people: in everyday life, on festive occasions and in the general system of culture where material and spiritual phenomena are inter-related and complementary.

The predominant orientation of the exhibition BULGARIA - TRADITION & BEAUTY is to present a comprehensive survey of the characteristics of traditional national costumes. The wealth of local and regional variants in the clothing is presented as they occur in various regions, districts and settlements on the historically differentiated territory of the Bulgarian people.

As regards the chronological boundaries, they comprise the period from the Bulgarian National Revival (18th-19th century) to the socialist revolution in 1944, although some customs and some of their elements can be traced almost as far back as the Middle Ages.

The main types of male and female traditional costumes are presented in their historical development with a view to the classification of clothing accepted in ethnography. According to their cut and to the way in which the women's clothes were worn, the women's costumes are differentiated in four groups: with two aprons, with one apron, *soukman* (low-cut sleeveless dress) and *saya* (a long dress), while men's costumes form two groups *belodreshna* (predominantly white clothes) and *chernodreshna* (predominantly black clothes).

Bulgarian national costumes have a complex composition resulting mainly from their functional purpose. The different living and working conditions, the natural environment and the season, the requirements of the family and calendar rituals, the aesthetic norms and many other factors have imposed relevant changes in the structure and composition of the costumes.

The shirt is the principal item in the composition of all varieties of national costumes. In addition to its more widespread name *riza*, in Western Bulgaria it is also known as *koshoulya.* In its material, form and ornamentation it is one of the most essential unifying elements in Bulgarian folk costume. It is made of linen or hemp cloth, whereas after the 19th century cotton fabric began to be used as well. It is a long garment, not cut at the waist, with long sleeves. During the early stages in the evolution of clothes, the shirt functioned simultaneously as an outer garment and as underwear, to which an apron was added for women, while men wore a belt with it. It occurs in two principal varieties according to the cut of the shirt, especially in its upper part, and according to its artistic ornamentation and in its differing geographic distribution. One of these variants is with shoulder yokes, and is gathered at the neck, the end of the sleeves and in their upper part. This type of shirt is known by the name of *burchanka* and it is usually associated with the women's costumes with two aprons, being very common almost all over the Danubian Plain, as well as in the northern foothills and slopes of the Balkan Range. The second variety is the tunic-like shirt which is associated only with the *soukman* and follows its geographic distribution.

The appearance of the costumes is determined above all by the outer garments. Depending on their cut, shape and place of attachment to the body, women's outer garments are fastened at the waist and resemble two aprons - one in front and one at the back - or they are fastened at the shoulders. The predominant forms of garments fastened at the shoulders are the *soukman* with its tunic-like cut and the *saya* - a dress that is open along its entire length in front. The *saya* is relatively less widespread. According to the appearance determined by the outer garments, women's costumes belong to the type of clothes that are open in their lower part, whereas men's costumes are clothes closed from below, as in the different forms of trousers - full-bottomed and tight-legged breeches *potouri* and *cheshiri.*

The belt is also an essential element of the costumes, because it performs a peculiar structurally-unifying role

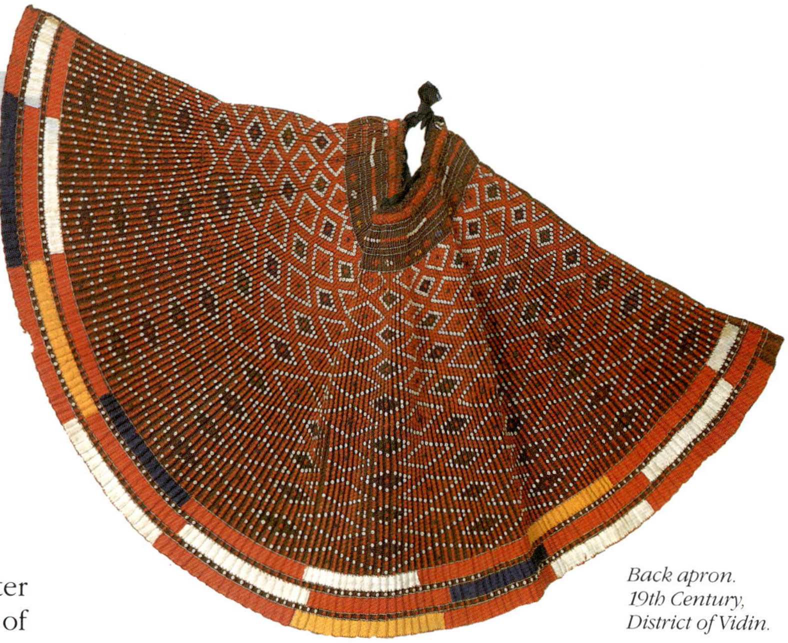

Back apron.
19th Century,
District of Vidin.

in the entire composition. It is tied around the outer garment. The belt is usually made of woollen cloth of either one colour, or in stripes of different colours. Usually it is in artistic harmony with the other elements of the costume, often being in a contrasting colour to the outer garment (*soukman or saya*). Another type of belt is knitted of black wool, long enough to be wound several times around the waist of the woman wearing it. This belt, which is more like a girdle, is often accompanied by a thin belt in the form of a decoratively woven band with ornamentation consisting of embroidery, and later also of beads. Unlike the girdle-belts, the narrow band-belts are short and they are fastened with metallic clasps. In addition to their direct function of holding the different items of the clothing in a unified composition, belts and girdles also function as markers of age and marital status. Usually unmarried girls do not wear belts and girdles. In some areas of the country the belt is associated with maternity. According to the requirements of tradition, it is tied on the wedding day (or on the day of the engagement) and is worn to the end of one's life.

The apron is also a typical and inseparable part in the total composition of the traditional women's costume and it has a clearly defined functional and aesthetic purpose. With its rich textile ornamentation, the apron is no longer an item of clothing with a practical or even constructive purpose and has become gradually a most prominent decorative focus which determines to the greatest extent the composition of the costume. In addition to the specific and richly artistic ornamentation, there is a wide variety of aprons performing different functions in life. The wearing of different types of aprons is determined by the age and the marital status of the person wearing them. Only young girls (below the age of 12-14 years) do not wear aprons, whereas maidens above 17-18 years of age, engaged girls and new brides wear aprons with a very rich ornamentation. During the wedding rite the bride necessarily wears two aprons, with red as the predominant colour of the ornamentation of the apron below and white for the apron over it.

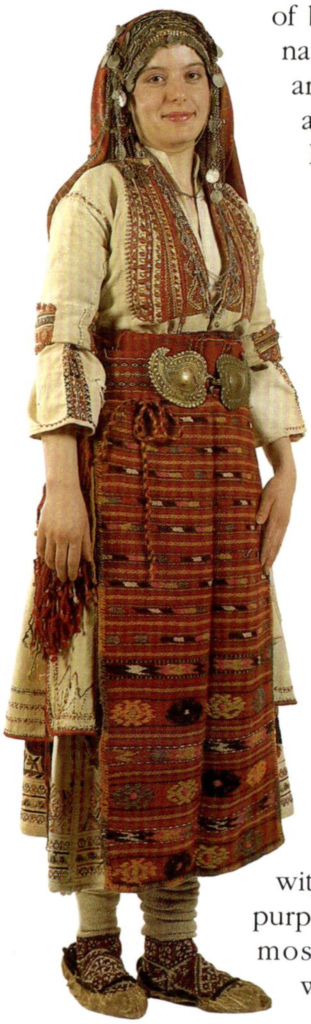

Young woman's festive costume (Saya dress),
second half of 19th Century. District of Sandanski.

The ancient outer garments, usually made of course homespun woollen cloth (*aba*), either black or white, manifest total stylistic unity with the remaining elements of the traditional clothing. They manifest an artistic approach that is typical of Bulgarian national costumes and consists of skilfully applied embroidery and braiding, as well as contrasting colours. The length of the outer garments is either below the waist or below the knees. The garments are open in front, often with skirts that become wider in their lower part, they can be sleeveless, or with long or short sleeves. The development of manufacturing in the second half of the 19th century resulted in their transformation. New variants were gradually created, which were made and decorated with factory-produced materials, although they did maintain a continuity with the older traditional forms in their colours, cut and length. While outer garments are an almost inseparable part of the men's costumes, in women's costumes they function mainly as festive or ritual elements. The different variants in the outer garments in traditional costumes are determined not only by the social and historical processes, but also by the different functions which they perform in the patriarchal life of the Bulgarians.

The older outer garments were associated directly with the age, sex and family structure of the traditional Bulgarian village. Irrespective of the natural and geographic environment or season, unmarried girls could not wear any other kind of garment except the sleeveless undecorated vest, whereas young brides were compelled to wear a fur coat or an ankle-length sleeveless coat made of white homespun woollen cloth (*aba*), with a wedge-like cut and a decoration consisting of braiding which is concentrated predominantly around the apices of the wedges. The ancient ritual wedding costume of the bride necessarily included an ankle-length outer garment (*djoube*) made of red silk or cotton, with stripes of a different colour, padded with cotton wool and held in place by numerous seams. During the wedding rite the bride also puts on a red coat made of red baize and trimmed with white lambs fur over the *djoube*. In some areas of the country the use of outer clothing followed the general Bulgarian traditions, according to which it was put on for the first time on the day of the wedding and was worn invariably for a definite period after the wedding, being stripped ritually on a special day stipulated by the respective custom.

The hairstyle and the way in which the headkerchief was worn are characteristic of the principles and norms typical of the universal Bulgarian tradition. Only unmarried girls could have a hairstyle showing the hair. After the wedding the hair was concealed by an elaborate bridal tying of the kerchief, with a special padding, hat, scarf and decoration for each region. Until the early years of this century, the exposed and representative maiden hairstyle consisted of numerous small braids starting around the forehead, framing the face and gathering in one or two big plaits that fall freely upon the girl's back. The wreath made of flowers, wheat straws or of beads and strings of coins, the braided hair ornament (*kosichnik*) and the nosegay were common additional elements to the hairstyle of young unmarried girls.

Compared with the hairstyle of unmarried girls, that of married women was much simpler, especially with advancing age. After the wedding, women completely concealed their hair under a special square or rectangular kerchief made of white hemp or linen

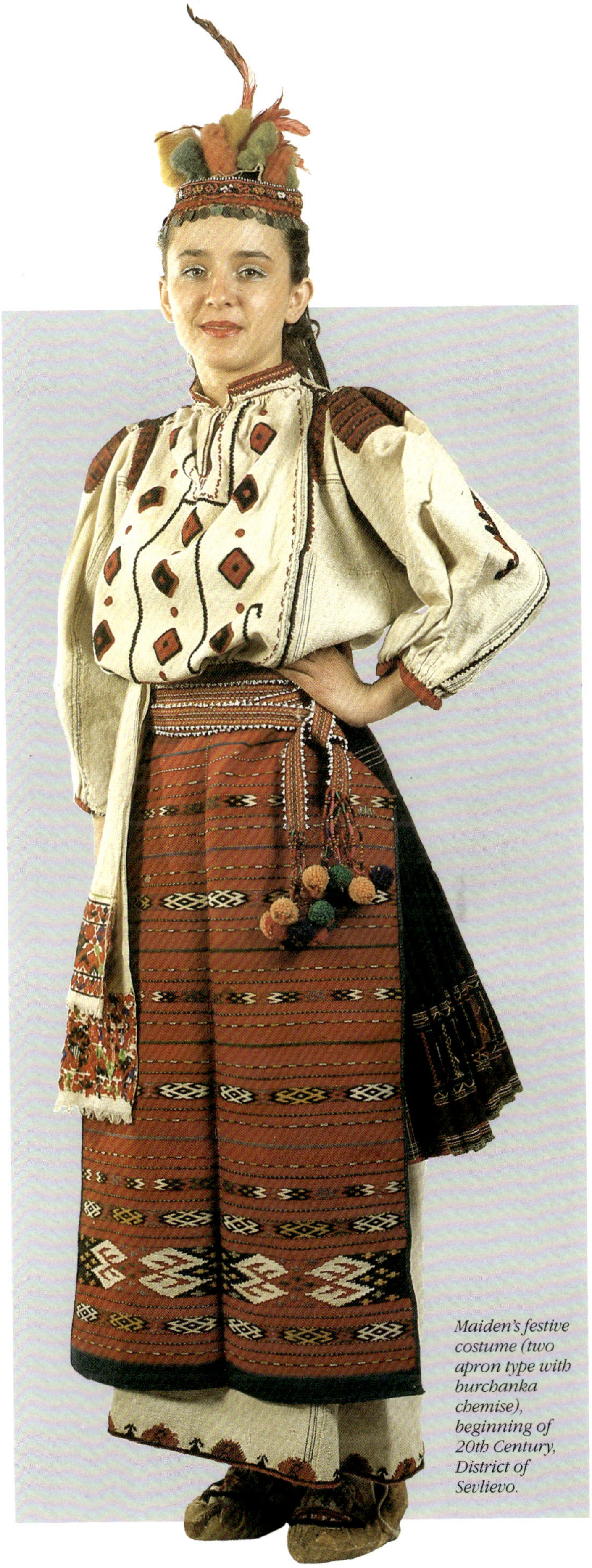

Maiden's festive costume (two apron type with burchanka chemise), beginning of 20th Century, District of Sevlievo.

Man and woman's (Soukman dress) festive costumes, end of 19th Century, Sofia.

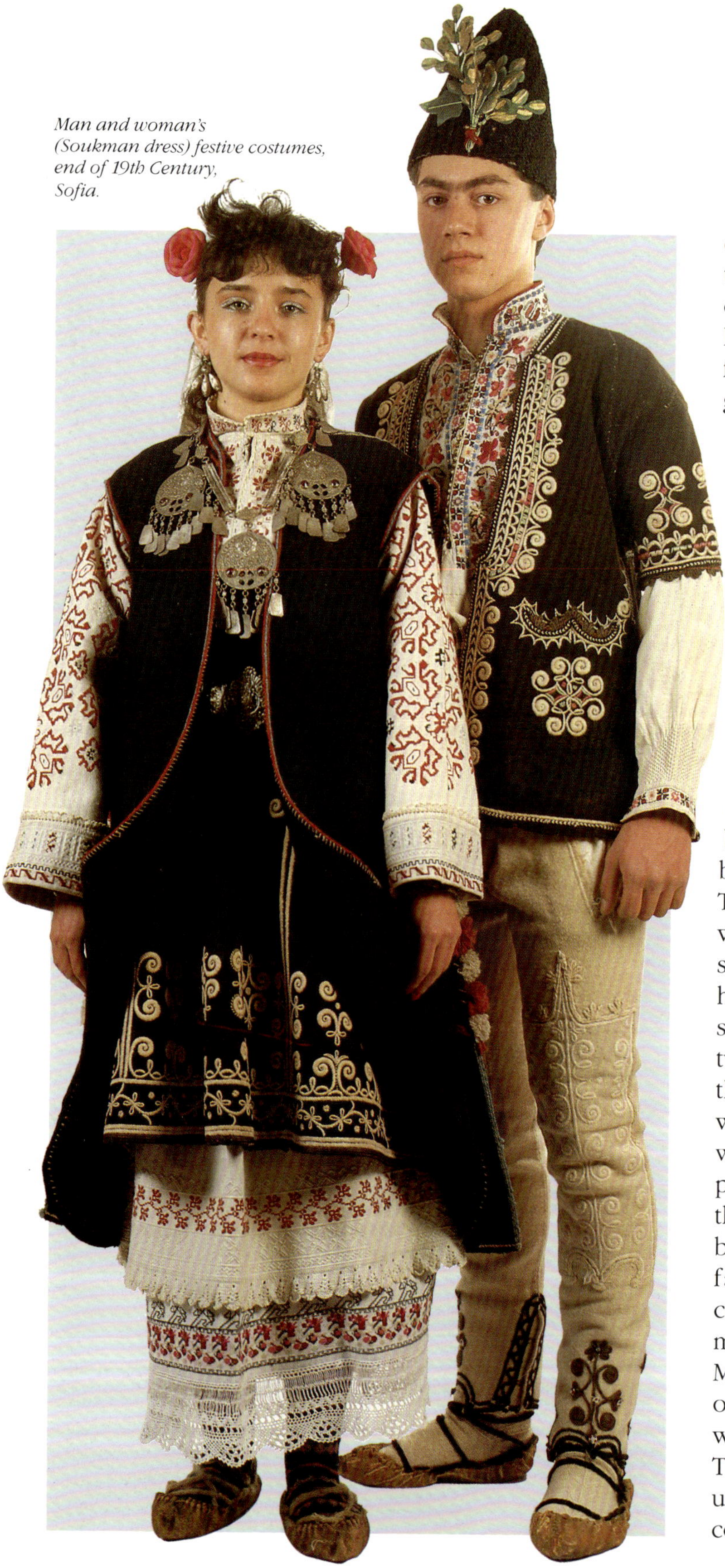

cloth, traditionally imposed as a compulsory marker of the married status of the woman. The kerchief is an element of the various styles whereby different hairstyles and articles of adornment attribute different forms to it. In most cases the ancient hairstyles were gradually replaced by artificial pads. However, the strictly observed taboo according to which the hair of a married woman was not to be exposed was preserved by tradition almost until the 1930s i.e. to the time which marked the end of the adherence to the main indicators of age and family status in the traditional national costumes.

The first bridal kerchief is associated with the ritual covering of the bride's head on the day of the wedding. The bride's ancient cover (or veil) was made of red woollen cloth, and very often it was made of a man's red girdle shaped like a hood and placed in front of the bride's face. Coins are sewn onto the veil where it touches the face and small bundles of golden (shiny) wire fall in front of the bride's eyes - clearly with an apotropaic significance. The veil made of the man's red girdle as a compulsory wedding attribute, and more specifically the red colour, symbolises the social affiliation of the bride to her husband's family and her perceived submissive and subordinate position. A wedding wreath made of a twisted vine or a wild rose branch by the girl-friends of the bride is placed over the red veil. The wreath is tied with red thread and is decorated with flowers and red wool shaped to resemble a cross. The most common practice is for this wreath to be ritually torn apart by the wedding guests during the wedding ritual. It may be preserved by the bridegroom's mother for the new family. The bridal tying of the headkerchief is complemented also by numerous trinkets made of metal, predominantly silver.

Maternity is indicated by a white kerchief worn low over the eyes, whereas widowhood imposes the wearing of a black kerchief tightly framing the face. The white kerchief is worn by Bulgarian village women until the old age, being gradually replaced by a coloured or black kerchief in some places.

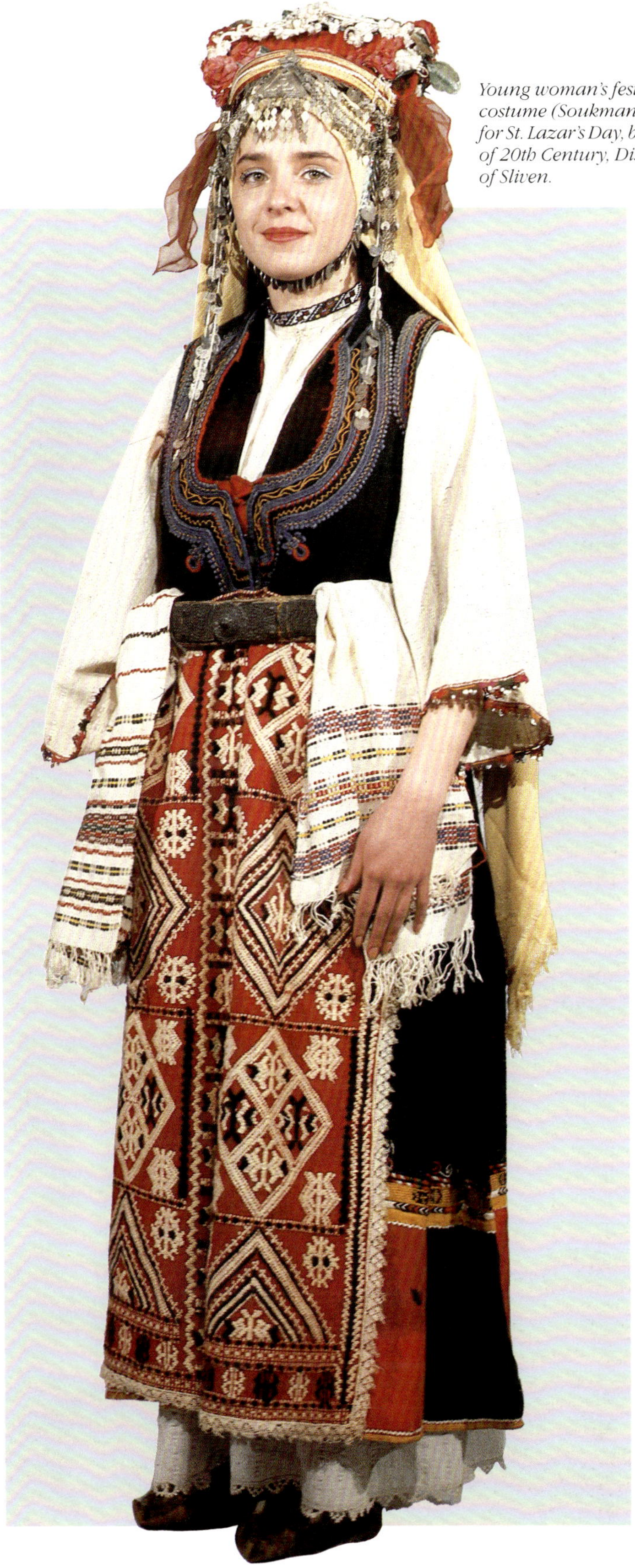

Young woman's festive costume (Soukman dress), for St. Lazar's Day, beginning of 20th Century, District of Sliven.

The hair of men, usually cut to the nape of the neck, or forming a forelock (*perchem or chombas*) until the end of the 18th century, was almost always covered too. The black (less frequently white) fur hat is an invariable element of the traditional Bulgarian men's costume, being even perceived as a national specificity and as an ethnically differentiating feature. In the more ancient traditional period in the development of men's clothing there is evidence about the wide use of felt hats which were later replaced by the fur caps. A red cap called *podkapnik* (either knitted or made of woollen cloth) was worn until very late and it was characteristically a main element of the men's costume of Western Bulgaria.

Feet were shod largely depending on traditional norms and on the climate. A very common practice was for the woman to go about barefoot for most of the year. In summer the unmarried girls danced the round dance (*horo*) also barefoot. Red leather slippers were worn only on holidays, red and yellow shoes made of soft leather were the privilege of brides only during the wedding ritual. A unifying element for Bulgarian national costumes can be seen in the leather sandals (*tsurvouli, opinki*), either pointed in front or rounded, sometimes boat-shaped, and tied with leather straps. Other common elements are the leggings and gaiters (*navoi, kaltsi* and *kaltsouni* resembling in shape boots of thrashed homespun cloth, as well as the knitted woollen socks with their specific ornamentation. Only the gaiters of the brides were made of white homespun woollen cloth with red braiding. When they went out, unmarried girls put on slippers, while married women wore red or black shoes (*kalevri* or *kondouri*). Shoes were among the compulsory ritual gifts that the bridegroom gave to the bride. The putting on of the shoes on the bride during the wedding was almost equivalent to the ritual tying of the kerchief on her head and of a belt round her waist.

Bulgarian national costumes were also enriched by a number of other accessories or articles of adornment, nosegays and kerchiefs which performed both decorative functions as markers of social relations. Such is the function of the ornamented kerchiefs that are part of the wedding costumes of the bridal couple and of the remaining ritual persons, for example the various kerchiefs tucked into the belt, wound around the neck and crossed in front of the chest. Throughout the entire wedding rite the hands of the bride are necessarily covered by a white towel with ornamented borders. The costume of the young girls participating in the rites on St.Lazarus' Day (the Saturday before Palm Sunday) is also complemented by many kerchiefs tucked into the belt, flying in the air "for good crops and fertility" during the vigorous Spring dances performed by the girls.

The artistic decoration consisting mainly of multicoloured embroidery and ornamented textile materials were prominent in the formation of traditional Bulgarian clothing. The decoration of the national costumes was the individual, non-specialised creativity of Bulgarian women and expressed their rich world outlook. The great variety of ornamental forms and harmonious colour combinations betray the unparalleled creative skills and the high aesthetic feeling of Bulgarian women, their expressions and their appreciation of beauty and harmony. What is more, their skill in making clothes attractive was of tremendous importance for their social prestige. The ornamentation on the national costumes was an inseparable part of the garment, organically linked with it, which determined the entire structure of the costume. The high artistic merits of traditional Bulgarian clothes, and above all of the women's costumes, have been attained by the skilful use of ornamentation consisting mainly of embroidery and textile decorative elements, and partly of artistic knitting, applique and braiding. These differing approaches to ornamentation have been used to different degrees in the individual items of clothing and costumes, and at the same time they contribute to the formation of the unique artistic originality of Bulgarian national clothes.

The strength of the impact of the colours of the ornamentation on the national costumes is determined not by the number of colours used for a certain combination, but by their correlation and the rich harmony of colours and nuances obtained by rhythmic alternation of the coloured stripes in the clothing or by the degree of saturation of the colours in the embroidered ornamentation. Vegetable dyes have also contributed substantially to the richness of the colours and for the variety of the artistic ornamentation, because they give different nuances to the colours. This explains why embroidered and textile ornaments belonging to the same regional type are at the same time identical and different, expressing the multi-variant character of Bulgarian national costumes.

The geometric ornament prevails in the decorative system of the clothing. It is applied either independently or in combinations with the stylised floral or animal figures, most often forming stripes. The lozenge or the square determines to the highest extent the geometric style of the ornamentation, with rectangular or triangular motifs occupying a secondary position. The composition of some embroidered patterns in the corners and along the borders of bridal headkerchiefs *oubrous* and *sokai* is characterised by the circle as a geometric figure, which suggests a clear semantic connection between these two motifs. The genesis of the geometric ornaments predominating in the decorative pattern should be derived undoubtedly from the primary ornamentation of the clothing, which can be traced back to the earliest stages of classless society.

Stylization of the floral ornament, which is most characteristic of the embroidered ornamentation of Bulgarian national costumes, is widely attested. Even when the motifs have been inspired by Nature (flowers, birds, animals and, more rarely, human figures), they are always rendered geometrically as a result of the complex evaluation of ornamental formation. In addition to the stylized floral ornament, the ornamentation of the costumes often features its freer variant, a motif closer to the prototype, presented most often by combinations of stripes with repeated, straight or twisted branches with flowers in full blossom or in

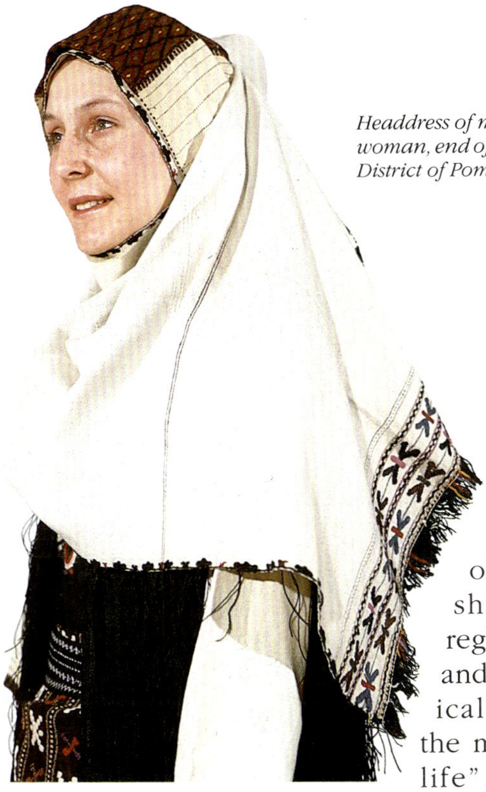

Headdress of married woman, end of 19th Century, District of Pomorie.

buds. This ornamental embroidery motif is typical of the ornamentation of many old women's shirts from many regions of the country and is probably thematically connected with the motif of the "tree of life" which was very popular in ancient art.

Stylized animals, birds and human figures appear in the ornamentation of the older costumes, mostly on the skirts of the women's shirts, on the aprons and on the outer garments. Although not so widespread as the geometric and floral ornaments, they also occupy a stable place in the Bulgarian ornamental patterns, notably in embroidery. Most elaborate and most interesting from the point of view of their semantic content are the embroidery compositions comprising a human figure. It is presented in a strongly reduced form and only individual details reveal a similarity with a human image. The schematically presented human figures are shaped in bands resembling structurally a round dance (*horo*).

Without being a decorative element of the clothing as, for example, the embroidery and the woven ornamentation, knitting also contributes to its aesthetic qualities. Most prominent among the knitted items of clothing are the woollen socks with their many colours, which are widespread throughout the entire ethnic territory. The knitted elements of the costume also comprise the *kaltsi* (gaiters covering the legs from the ankles to below the knees), *narukvitsi* which covers the arms from the wrist to the elbow, gloves, mittens, various crochet laces trimming the sleeves and the skirts of the women's shirts, the artistically knitted apron ties, decorative laces, etc. Artistic knotting and crochet work correspond stylistically to the textile and embroidered ornamentation. There is even a process whereby homemade laces - either needleworked or crocheted - gradually began to substitute the decorative functions of embroidery and textile woven ornamentation of the clothes, with the typical distinction that needlework was more frequently used in urban women's clothes, while the crocheted ornamentation continued to adorn the traditional village costumes.

Applique ornamentation on the clothing played an important aesthetic role. It was widely used as a decorative motif on women's clothes, mainly on *soukmans* and *sayas*, less on outer garments. Applique ornaments were most frequent on leather clothes, especially on the fur jackets worn by women in combination with the two-apron costume. The decorative interpretation of the applique ornamentation betrays a clear aspiration to form an integral costume composition and not to intensify any one external artistic effect.

Another characteristic approach to the ornamentation of Bulgarian national costumes consists of the wide use of trimming with braids of different colours to emphasise the ends and the connecting seams of the thick upper garments. The composition of the ornamentation with braiding is based predominantly on the principle of colour contrast. Against the background of the black, white or striped coloured cloth of the garment the combinations of solid black, red or orange braided stripes stand out very clearly and it is they that determine the actual regional artistic originality of the costumes.

Nations are differentiated from one another and learn about one another to this day by the numerous and varied forms of their traditional costumes. They are the visible material symbol of the national specificity, but at the same time they also contribute to communications and cultural synthesis among the different nations. This is so because with its specific ethnic properties the traditional clothing of every nation has also preserved many common features that are inherent to the culture of several, many or all nations.

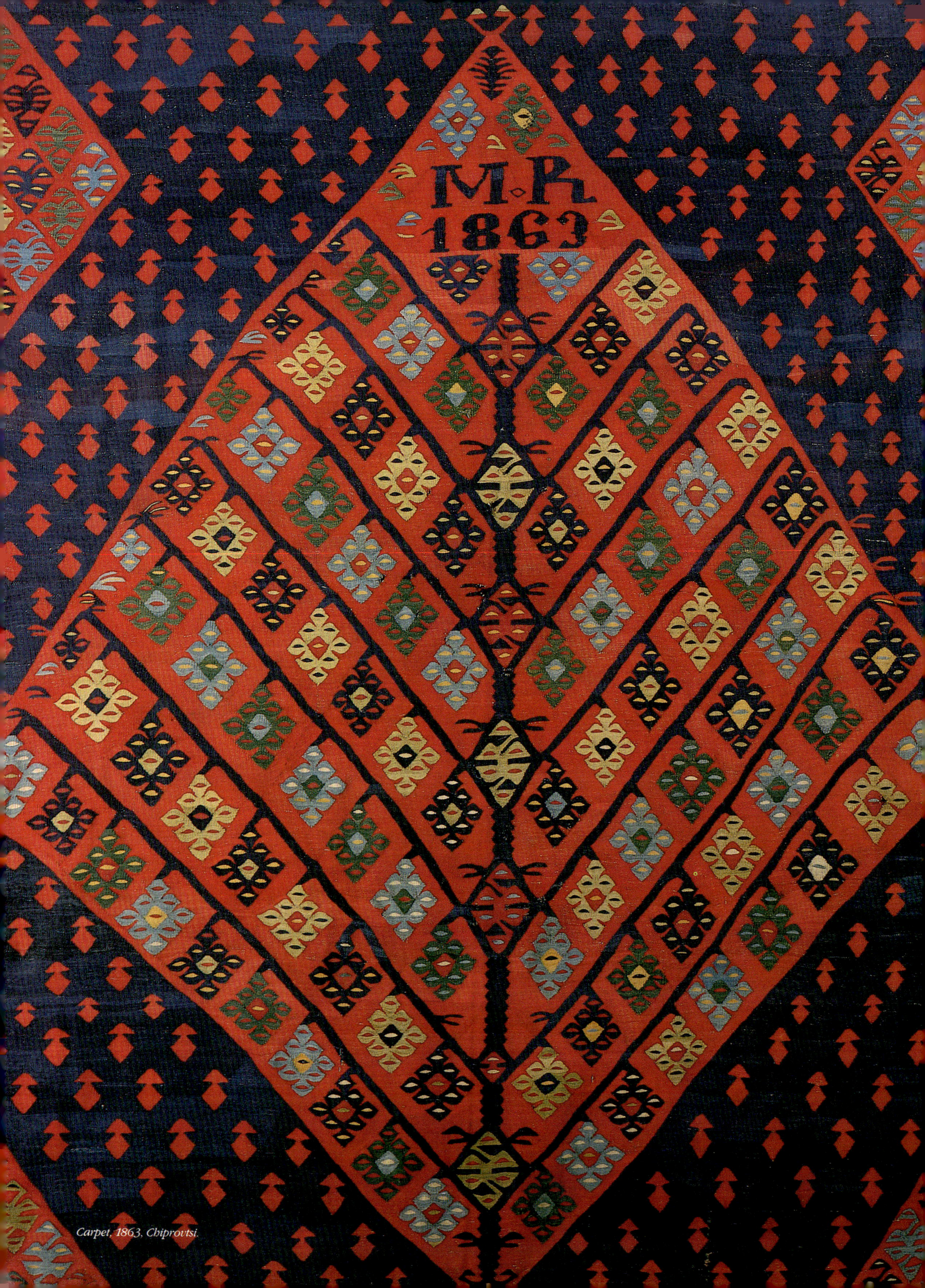

Carpet, 1863, Chiprovtsi.

Textiles

Maria Sarafova

Weaving is a sphere of our traditional material culture where the woman, traditionally occupied with indoor activities , has the leading role and finds favourable opportunities for demonstrating her skills. Having learned to perfection, as a result of a rich heritage, the practical and artistic properties of textiles, women produce diverse fabrics. They make good use of the properties of the textile material in order to create suitable, hard wearing and beautiful textiles, according to their function. All activities related to weaving are performed by women, at home, using wooden, often primitive, tools.

By the loom the woman supplies her family with fabrics, necessary for the clothing of its members (homespun, cotton, linen, aprons, waist-bands), for arranging the house (rugs, goat's hair covers, tufted rugs, carpets), for household use (table-cloths, pieces of cloth, towels, bags, sacks, baby slings). Textiles are also used in rituals. In many regions of the country the bride and the bridegroom walk along white material or rugs to the gate of the bridegroom's house. The wagon with the bride's dowry is covered with a patterned rug. Ritual persons and wedding-guests are presented with towels, chemises and bags. At a funeral a dead person's body is covered with white material.

These are mainly things of wide practical usage, satisfying everyday needs. Taking into consideration their main function, the weaver strives to produce pretty articles which delight the eye and make the home look comfortable. Items of utilitarian nature are turned into works of art. In the decoration of textile the Bulgarian woman expresses her feelings, emotions and dreams, as well as ideas of beauty and harmony.

By the amount and the quality of the woven material one can determine the skill and industry of Bulgarian women as well as their aesthetic sense. The folk concept of the laborious maiden is based on her ability to spin and weave. The trousseau which the bride brings to her new home is often thought to be a sign of her industry and her virtues.

The adoption by the Bulgarians of the weaving techniques and experience is a centuries-old process, bearing traits of complex interaction between different cultures. The inherited textiles, weaving tools, techniques and their names testify to a long-lived and highly-developed weaving culture.

Brought from the lands of the Slavs and Proto-Bulgarians, and enriched by ancient local and Eastern influences, this tradition developed and continued to exist in the years of foreign political oppression. It is not by chance that together with the general national revival in 18th and 19th centuries this folk art also flourished. The textiles in the exhibition in Liverpool Museum are specimens of that period.

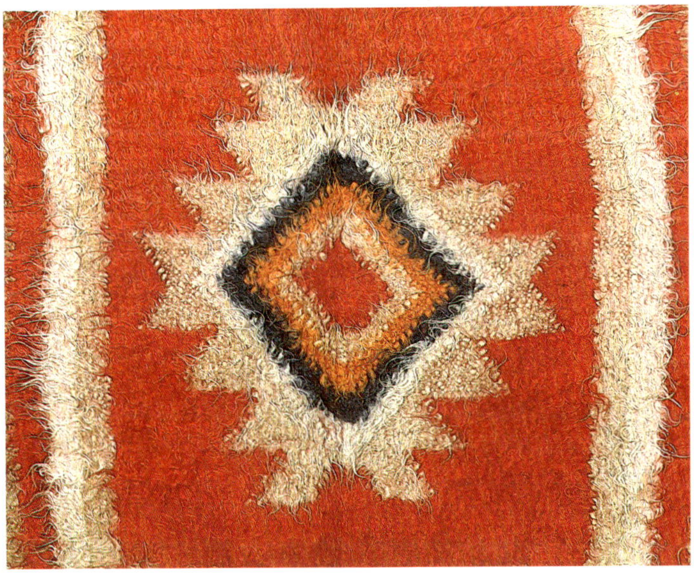

Tufted rug (kitenik), 19th Century, Sliven.

Home weaving is mainly done on a horizontal loom. Two main weaving techniques are used; sleazy and fourfold. On a vertical loom, brought from the East, were woven the Bulgarian carpets, widely known in the Turkish Empire for their high quality.

While weaving, the Bulgarian woman uses yarn of animal origin (fleece) and to a lesser extent goat's hair. Less common are the fabrics made of vegetal fibres such as hemp and flax. These materials were well known to the Slavs and to the Thracians. Sericulture

(silk-worm breeding) is also centuries old. It provided silk as a raw material for home weaving. In the 19th century cotton too became a raw material, partly substituting for hemp and flax.
Folk weavers know the dyeing properties of plants. They know how to obtain dyes from them and thus create exceptionally rich colour design in their fabrics. The variety of colours and hues is obtained not only from various dyeing substances, but from the different density of the dyes when dyeing. In order to stabilise the colours, various stabilisers are used, usually from vegetal or mineral origin (pear or cabbage juice, mud from under a grindstone, and cinder).
Much textile production is devoted to small fabrics (aprons, waist bands, belts, cushions, towels, bags, babies' clothes, table-cloths). They are used for clothing, in the interior of the house, and in the everyday life of the family. The application of various weaving techniques brings to them great diversity and richness of pattern. A decoration using the striped pattern is a common characteristic in the textiles of all Slavonic people. It is distinguished by the rhythmic arrangement of the stripes and colour. The geometrical pattern is predominant and considered to be antique. Its combination with motifs of birds, animals, human figures and vegetal ornaments in an integrated composition contributes to the high, artistic value of these textile works.
A substantial part of home-weaving is given to the production of textiles used for the interior arrangement of the house; rugs, tufted rugs ("gouberi" and "halishta") goat's hair covers and carpets. They are an inseparable part of the interior of every Bulgarian house. They are used for covering the floor or as a covering when sleeping. Having a wide use, the rug is broadly spread through-out the country. It is woven on a horizontal loom and is used for both spreading and covering.

Rug, 19th – 20th Century, District of Gotse Delchev.

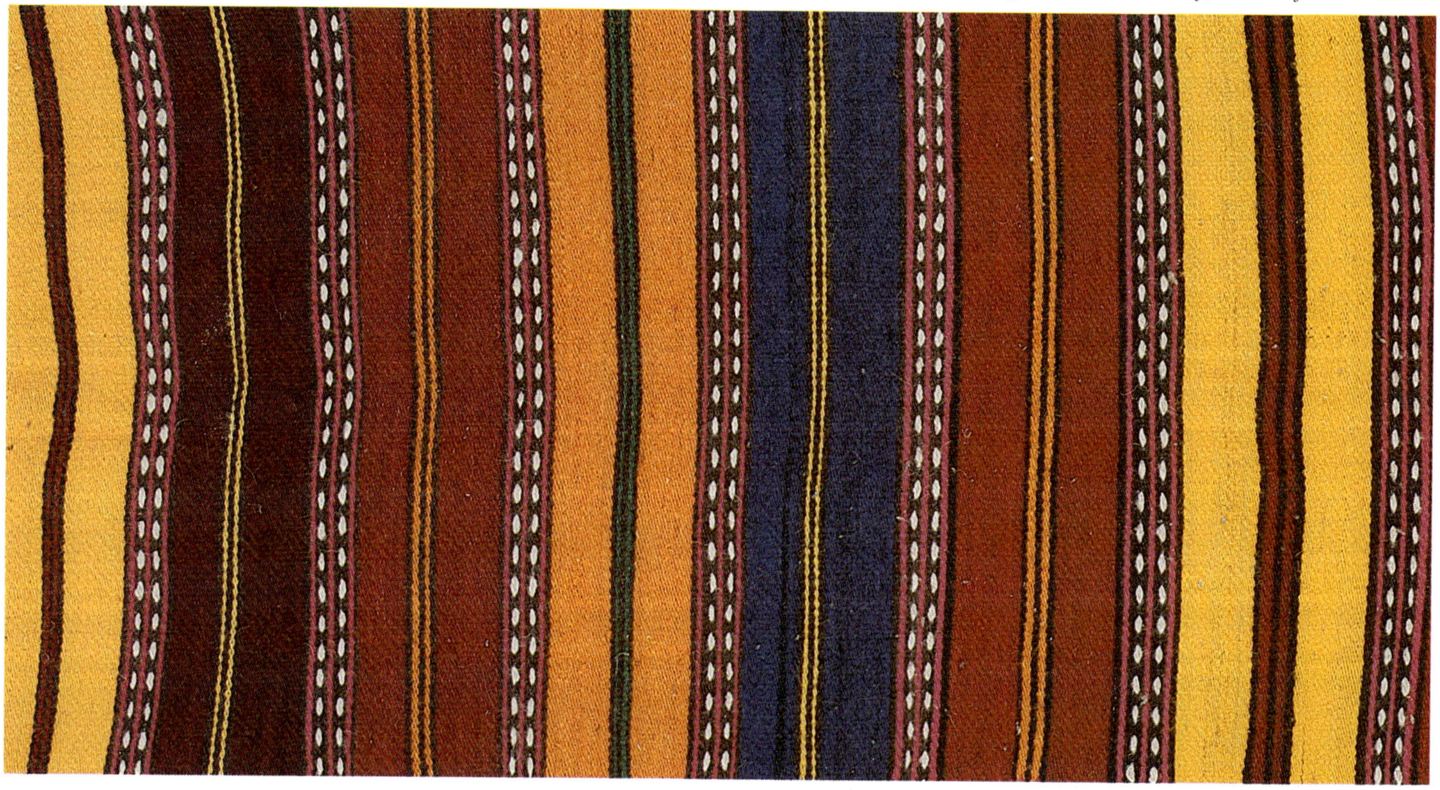

Felt textile, end of 19th Century, Koprivshtitsa.

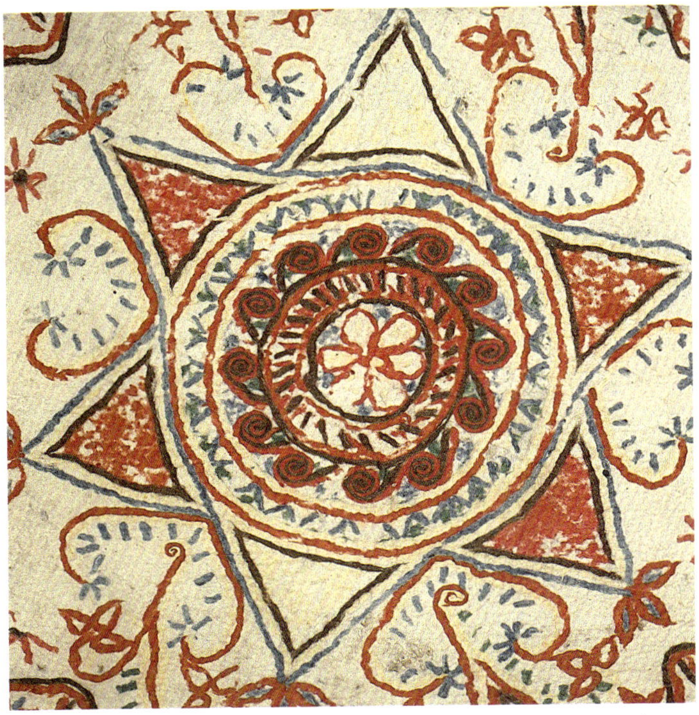

The antique patterns are made of wool, goat's hair,and hemp in their natural colours; white, beige, brown and grey. At a later stage appear the *"variegated rugs"*. Their decoration is of linear pattern, with alternation of stripes of different colours and strictly observed symmetry. The sense of selection and combination of colours and hues is essential. The colour harmony of the variegated rug is its greatest value. The red, green, white and black colours predominate, whereas blue and yellow are not so frequent. The colour combinations are specific for the different regions of the country which makes distinguishing them easy, (the main variants deriving from Turnovo, Gabrovo, Kjustendil, Samokov, and Koprivshtitsa).

The spread of the *carpet-type rug* is a recent phenomenon. Its production is mainly concentrated in the towns of Sliven, Teteven, Samokov, Karlovo, Kotel, Kalofer, and Pirin mountain. Its composition is allied to the linear, rhythmic design of the variegated rug, the only difference being the tearing up of the weft into separate motifs in stripes of diverse colours. The decorative design of the carpet-type rug is mid-way between the rug and the carpet. In spite of its close relationship to the carpet it is externally different from it - the warp either faintly showing or invisible. It is used for covering floors or window seats. Carpet-type rugs are woven on a horizontal loom.

There are records of the carpet industry in Bulgaria, dating back to 17th century. No earlier records are available. It can only be assumed that the carpet industry was known as the Proto-Bulgarians who were in contact with the culture of the people of the Caucasus. During the 18th and 19th century, at the time of National Revival the industry expanded into a rapidly developing craft with a broad market in the lands of the Turkish Empire.

The carpets made by the Bulgarian carpet-weavers were highly appreciated and sought after as they were known for the strength of their fabric and the fastness of their colours. The richness of their pattern ranks them as pieces of art. They are woven on a vertical loom in smooth (double-faced) technique. According to the colour combination and ornamental design there are two types of carpets: West Bulgarian, made in the mountain regions of Chiprovtsi and Samokov and East Bulgarian with the town of Kotel as the centre.

With respect to composition and ornamental design the Chiprovtsi carpets are more varied. They are typified by their small geometrical motifs, regularly distributed, as well as by their compositions of stylized pictures of plants, animals, objects and human figures. Their colour design is also rich and based on the colour contrast between a principal tone as a background (dark-blue, red, beige) and the variety of hues in the construction of motifs.

The Kotel carpets are characterized by their strict geometrical figures, rhythmically distributed by colour and form. The arrangement of ornaments is done in horizontal,vertical and diagonal rows. The blue, green, red and brown colours are prevalent.

As coverings in the Bulgarian house the *tufted rugs* (*"kitenitsi", halishta"*) are used. In some places their production was intended for the market. Most tufted rugs are produced in the Rhodopes, in the towns of Kotel, Sliven, Yambol, Gabrovo, Elena, and Koprivshtitsa. They are woven out of yarn or tufts of wool, unicoloured, of striped design or a combination of field and warp. The decorative motifs of this kind of textile fabric are large, with rough and indistinct outlines because of the structure of the material.

Another kind of home-made fabrics are *the goat's hair rugs and the covers*. They are used for coverings when sleeping, especially in the mountain regions of the country. They are either unicoloured or in multicoloured stripes. As a decorative device weavers often used the displacement of stripes when sewing up the separate pieces. A later development is a decorative composition with a centre and a frame. The old-fashioned goat's hair rugs are made in the natural colours of the goat's hair, whereas in the recent products the colour is deep. The Rhodopes region is famous for its coloured goat's hair rugs. Their essential colours are red, orange, green and yellow. The combinations of these colours reflect the wearer's perception of the surrounding landscape.

In some regions of the country another kind of textile covering is used, namely *felt*. It is part of the Proto-Bulgarian heritage. It is an unwoven textile and has limited usage in Strandja mountain and in some sub-Balkan countries. It is primitively made, its technology being that of hot felting, that is, a rolled layer of wool in natural colour is soaked with hot water and is beaten with a cudgel in order to make it mat and compact. It is decorated with coloured stripes of wool which are arranged on the basic layer and which adhere to it during the hot felting.

Its decorative pattern is developed in parallel stripes along the length of the material or in a rectangular field with a frame around it. It is ornamented by geometrical figures and vegetal motifs, and bears the signs of the techniques used in manufacture.

In spite of the influx of factory made textiles into everyday life and the effects of urbanisation reducing the usage of home-made textiles, weaving has been kept alive during the post-liberation period.

The tradition of home-weaving is still practiced today and its patterns give a special national colouring to the interior of the modern Bulgarian house.

Rug with carpet pattern, 19th Century, Sliven.

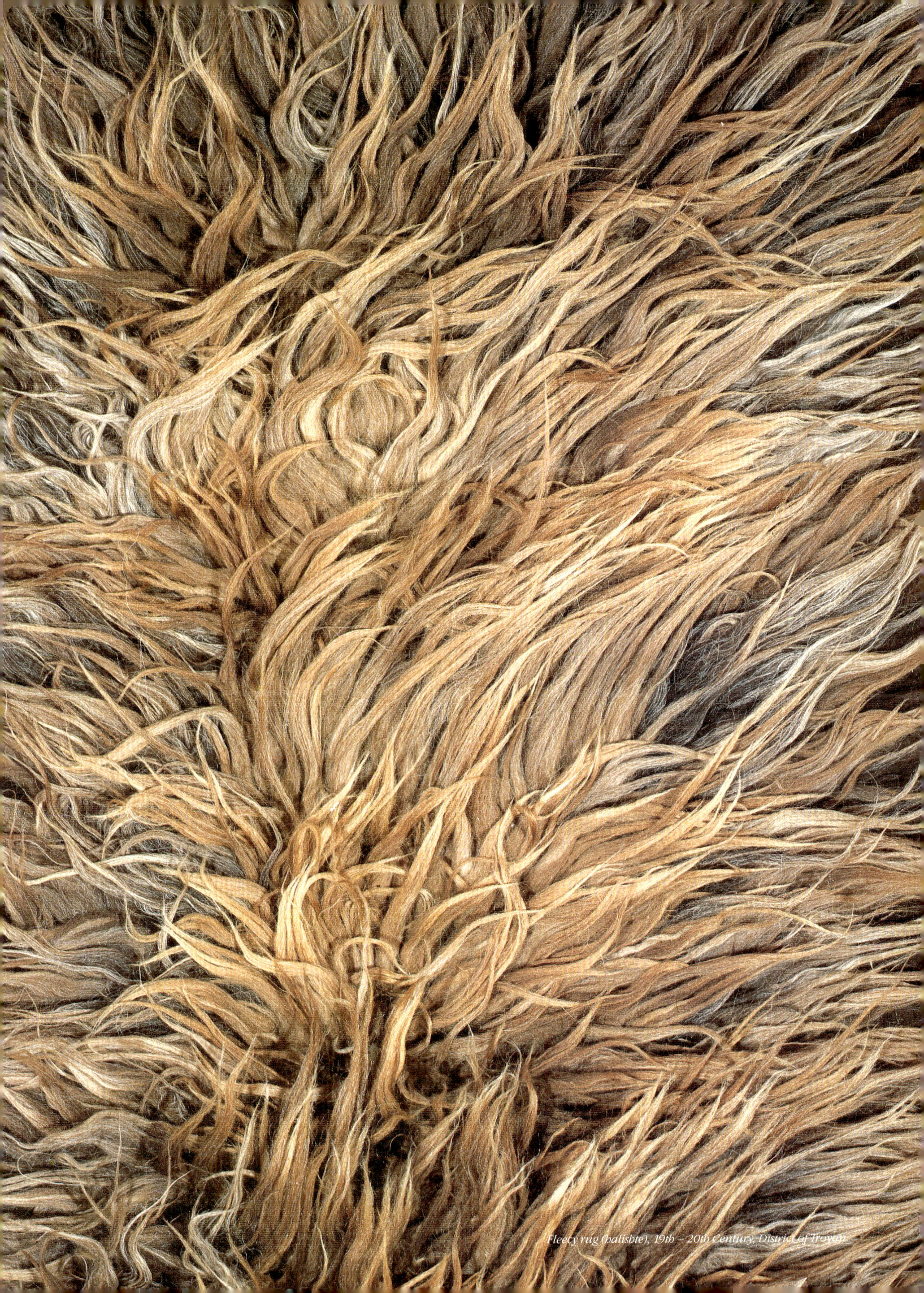

Fleecy rug (halishte), 19th – 20th Century, District of Troyan.

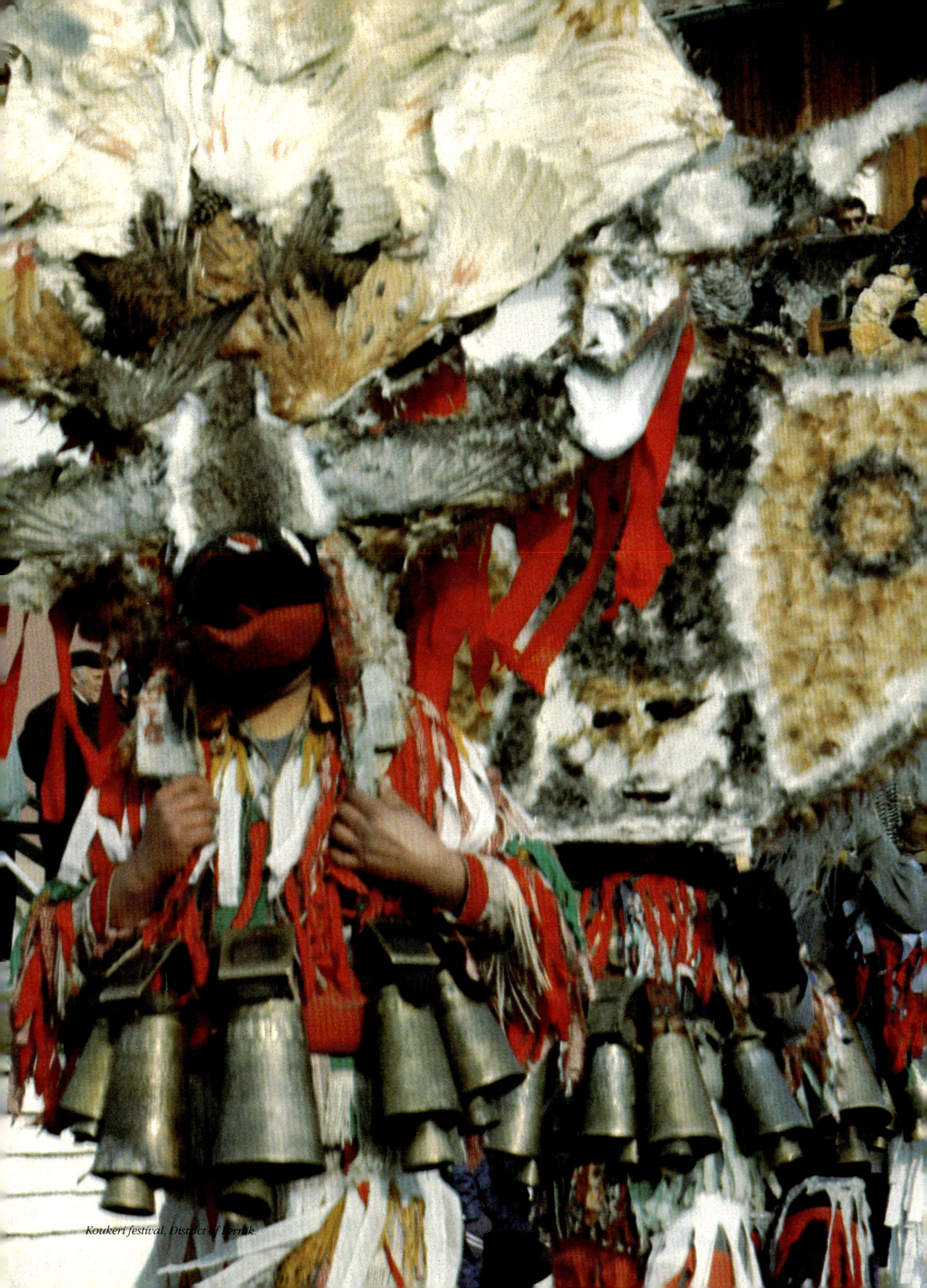

Koukeri festival, District of Pernik.

Folk Traditions

Ignat Minkov

Traditions are an unchanging and socially inherited feature in the development of every society, a mechanism for the preservation and the handing down of social information from one generation to the next. Moreover, of particular importance for the continuity of this process is the content of that which is being passed to posterity and its ability to satisfy the needs of those who are receiving the cultural heritage. A number of other factors also contribute to the social continuity of traditions. These factors act together to form the specificity of the process in each individual country and social community.

In Britain, for example, many elements of the traditional way of life were eliminated as early as in the 17th-18th century during the Industrial Revolution in the country. In Bulgaria this took place much later, and even today, many of the oldest generation of Bulgarians have preserved memories about the way of life of their fathers and forefathers. Many of the social interactions typical of the ordinary people under conditions of pre-industrialized labour have been preserved, and here they are defined most generally as the traditional way of life.

The historical proximity of these times whose cultural values are being inherited today, has resulted in the enrichment of the scope and content of the cultural heritage. This is because there are still many channels through which this heritage can be seen as relevant and be accepted by the people of today.

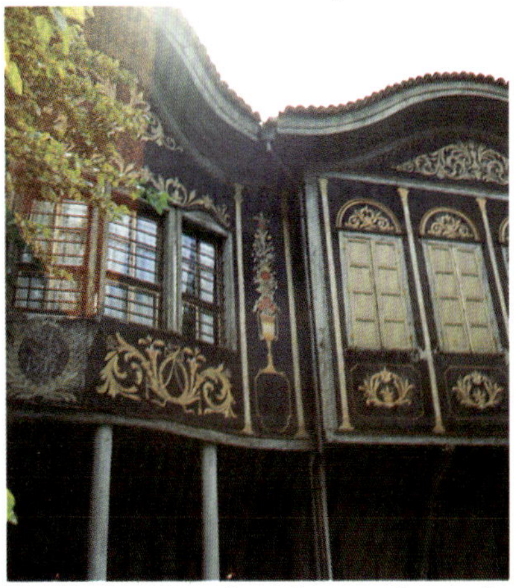

Traditional house from the Revival. Now the Ethnographical Museum in Plovdiv.

Taking into account the variety of forms through which traditional cultures can penetrate modern times, we shall focus attention only briefly on those of them that are actively manifested and have obvious ethnographic relevance to Bulgarian culture and mentality.

Today the old sections of the towns of Veliko Turnovo, Plovdiv, Gabrovo, Tryavna, Elena, Kotel and Lovech, as well as entire settlements as Bozhentsi, Koprivshtitsa and Kovachevitsa, are restored exactly as they looked during the National Revival period. They are adapted so as to meet some modern requirements of everyday life, without, however, changing their architectural appearance. Many of the buildings are used as museums and art galleries and as places for rest and recreation for artists, musicians, writers and film-makers. In the village of Bozhentsi and in some other places, old houses from the National Revival period are offered as part-time or full-time residences to writers and to other eminent figures of culture.

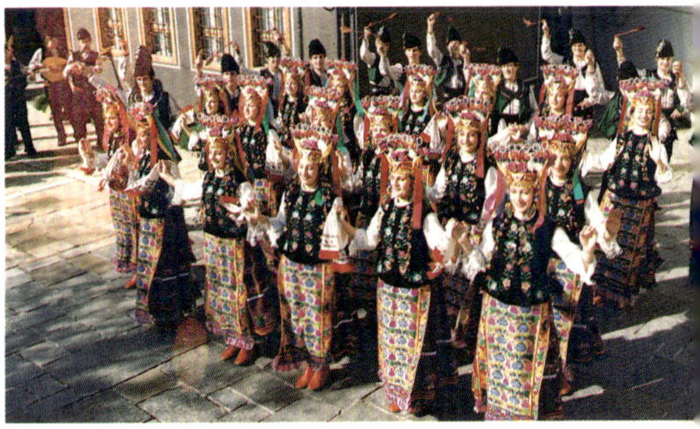

Folk group performance, old town of Plovdiv.

It is difficult to determine the cultural effect of the preservation of these monuments and of the active contact with them. Today they have become the focus of the festive and cultural life of the settlements. They have restored the historical atmosphere of the Bulgarian town or village and have become an important carrier of the historical record, preserving the natural environment of important political events. The very concern and care about them represent a positive social attitude.

Another aspect, their cultural and aesthetic impact, is seen in their architectural appearance. An example of this is the rational construction of the residential environment and of the houses themselves, with the skilful utilization of vertical space and the combination of mobile and immobile furniture with the enormous variety of architectural decoration. These and many other features of the inherited

Bulgarian house not only serve as examples to be followed in organizing the interior of the modern Bulgarian home, but also in the development of modern Bulgarian architecture and for consolidating its national specificity and colour.
Other forms of this inheritance can be seen in the traditions of home weaving which are still alive today in many regions of the country, predominantly among the rural population. Traditional textiles which would be suitable for the modern Bulgarian interior decoration are creatively restored. It is a universal practice to use Bulgarian national embroidery as a decorative element for various everyday materials: tablecloths and table-mats, towels and various items of clothing, introducing many new elements that have been imposed by the requirements of the modern age.
The aspirations to preserve and to include in everyday life masterpieces of the traditional folk culture - copper vessels, wrought iron, ceramic vessels and textiles, have gradually resulted in the restoration of many of the traditional crafts which are clearly of national and artistic character. The best artists and craftsmen working in this sphere are united today in the Union of Masters of Folk Arts and Crafts, established as an artistic organization in 1967. They are entrusted with the responsible task of preserving, restoring and developing the traditions of the old Bulgarian folk arts and crafts, organizing these activities in the form of production technology sessions and the production of sample pieces.
Owing to the active work of the Union of Masters of Folk Arts and Crafts, many folk traditions have been preserved in the sphere of metal processing and work with textiles, leather, fur and wood for making objects for daily use and ornamentation in Bulgarian folk style.
It should also be pointed out that not only are there folk masters, other craftsmen and producers, but also the many amateur weavers, embroiderers, woodcarvers and blacksmiths. They manufacture in original or slightly modified form, many objects for their own personal needs and as gifts for friends.
It would be interesting to study the spheres of life in which the specimens of traditional material culture and their new functions find application. Today they are not so much a symbol of the continuation of the traditional practices in the furnishing and interior decoration of the Bulgarian home and the organising of everyday life, interrupted by the dynamic processes of urbanisation as the counterpoint for the standardization and unification of the present-day material culture, accompanying the modernization of life. In the modern interior the traditional object introduces the sense of wellbeing of something made by the human hand, the national colour and originality, or it may assume a purely decorative function. It is not accidental that these processes are particularly intensive among the hereditary urban environments and among the urban intelligentsia. International tourism also has a very strong impact, unfortunately not always positive, because a special souvenir industry has developed for satisfying its needs.
These aspirations among our contemporaries to create for themselves an environment with objects made of natural materials symbolizing the way of life clearly following the laws of nature are of prime importance today in investing a meaning into the free time of the people, urging them to use it for individual expression and creativity, as well as for the preservation of the

Festival of Roses.

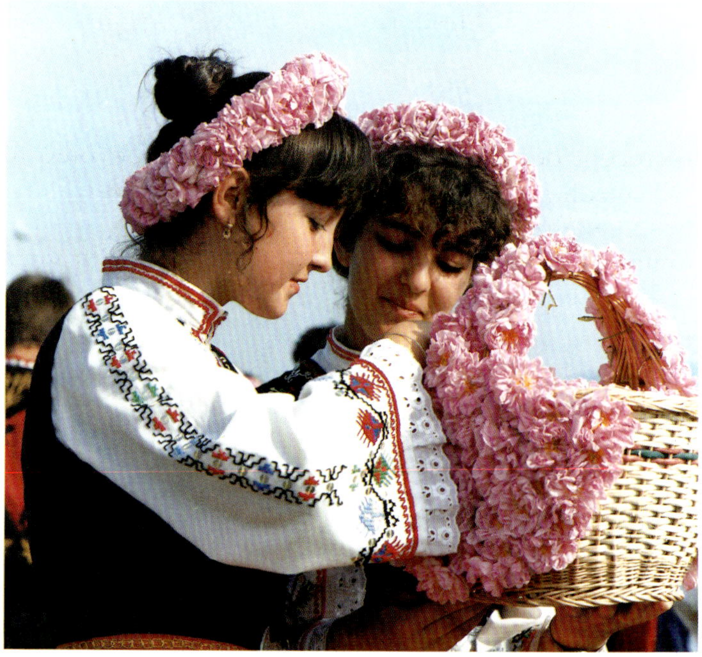

traditional virtues of the Bulgarian.

In recent decades increasing attention is devoted to folk medicine, to treatment with medicinal plants and to some other practices of folk healers, stripped of their irrational elements. They are being studied with great care by a specialized body set up by the Ministry of Public Health and Social Welfare, and every possible support is given to those healers who have proved their ability and gift of healing. In this case it is very important to assimilate the rich heritage of folk culture in this field and to bring all its rational elements closer to the modern social practice.

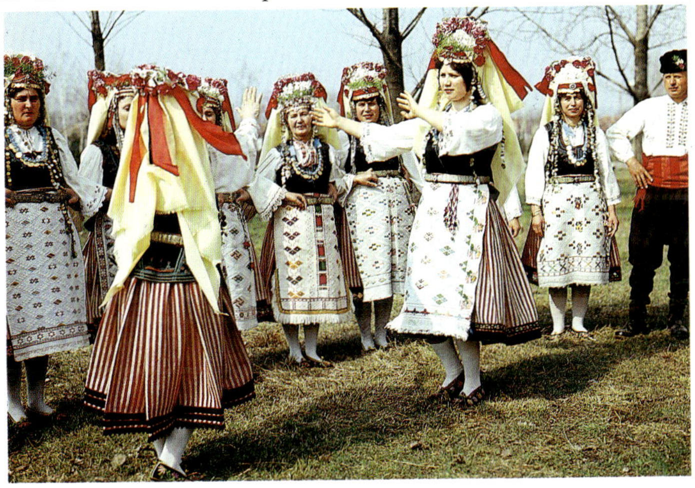

Lazarka ritual dance, District of Yambol.

Such a message from the past is perceived today in many elements and characteristics of traditional folk culture: the festive and ritual practices, the musical, song and dance folklore. The Bulgarian song and dance folklore enjoys the greatest interest today, especially among the population connected with the village life and from the regions where it has preserved for long its vitality: Thrace, the Rhodopes, Dobroudja and Western Bulgaria. Folklore occupies a central place in amateur art activities as it is an historically ingrained phenomena in this country of amateur (unprofessional) participation on a mass scale in various forms of art: songs, music, danciang, drama and painting.

The resurgence of interest in Bulgarian folklore in recent years (three or four decades) was largely due also to the broadcasts of Bulgarian radio and TV, to the activities of the nearly thirty state ensembles for folk songs and dances, and naturally to the apostolic work for a century and a half of ethnographers, folklorists and other collectors who have found and preserved hundreds of thousands of folk songs and tunes, festive folk dances, rituals and games.

Today, this practically inexhaustible source of national morale and aesthetics offers the miraculous life-giving water to the thirsty person of today. In addition to the very widespread participation in concerts and various programmes for entertainment on various festive occasions and the performing of folk songs in the family and among friends, the greater interest in folklore was particularly due to the village fairs, festivities and festivals of folk creativity. These have been organized periodically as local, regional or national festive occasions since the late 1950s. Tens of thousands of performers and spectators gather at some of them: the song contest at Rozhen, in the Rhodopes, the folkloric festivities "Pirin Is Singing", "Beautiful Thrace is Singing and Dancing" in Haskovo, the children's folklore festival "Rossen Zdravets" (Dew-Sprinkled Wild Geranium) and dozens of other events organized regularly at intervals of two to three years.

Since 1965 the National Festival of Folklore has been organized every five years in the town of Koprivshtitsa. The Festival has become a real national festive occasion of Bulgarian traditional folk culture. The best singers, instrumentalists, dancers, story-tellers, folklore ensembles and groups for folk customs participate in it. The various events preceding the last and fifth festival in Koprivshtitsa in 1986 involved the participation of over half a million people, part of whom are organized into 26,294 folklore ensembles and ritual groups. Observations have shown that in recent years there has been growing interest in the sources of authentic folklore and ritual practices, unaffected by later influences, which have preserved the elements of traditional culture in its purest form. A welcome fact in this respect is the participation of children on a wider scale, which is evidence that the cultural heritage is being perceived ever more actively by the youngest generation of Bulgarians.

On the initiative of the public organizations and with the active co-operation of specialists (ethnographers and folklorists), a large part of the traditional festive and ritual practices and symbols, forgotten somewhat in the first post-war decades, are again entering the Bulgarian festive calendar. This is valid both of the family holidays and of festive occasions devoted to various labour activities and connected with the annual natural cycle. Naturally, this inheriting of traditions is parallelled by a transformation of the ideas they carry. Thus, for instance, the earlier ritual practices during family holidays (weddings, christenings, entering a new home), which are being restored today, have lost some of their original sematic content and are perceived today mainly as beautiful symbols of welfare in the family, and of relations among kinfolk, neighbours and colleagues.

An entirely new content is also found in the revised ancient festive events like the carnivals of the *sourvakari* (children going from house to house to wish a Happy New Year by tapping the back of the people with a decorated cornel twig), the *koukeri* (mummers), the various spring rites and the maiden games on St. Lazarus' Day (the Saturday before Palm Sunday). They are no longer perceived as a means of chasing the evil forces away or of guaranteeing marriage for someone or the coming of Spring. Instead they appear simply as a beautiful and attractive group and as a village festival, full of ancient symbolism, bringing joy and happiness and contributing to closer ties among people, to the consolidation of the friendly and neighbourly relations in the entire village community. The old fairs and festivities in the villages are being restored with the same objectives in mind.

Many old traditional festivities and holidays have served today as the basis for modern festive events which reflect the work of the people. For example, the traditional holiday *Trifon zarezan*, previously dedicated to St. Tryphon, the patron saint of wine-growers, is already celebrated as the Day of Wine-

Sourvaknitsa (decorated cornel twig), Distrct of Karnobat.

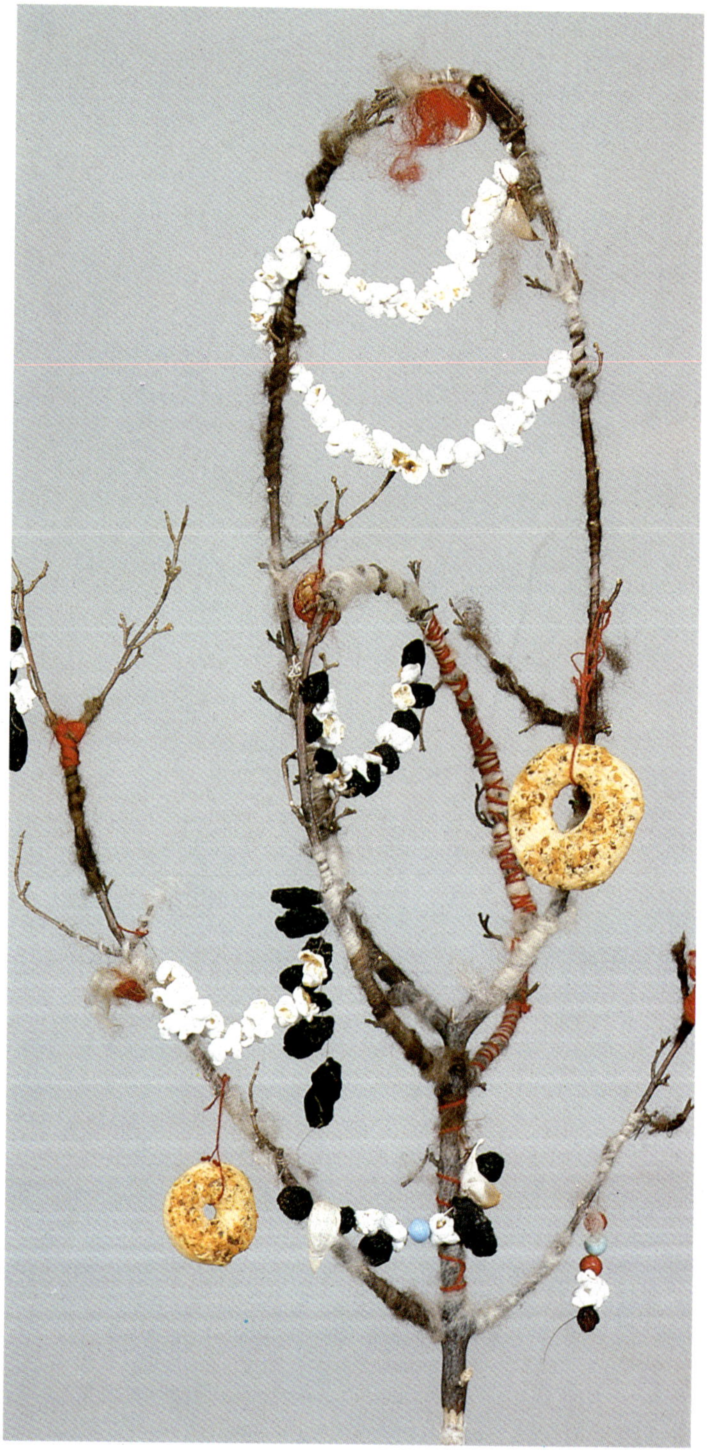

Koukeri festival, District of Pernik.

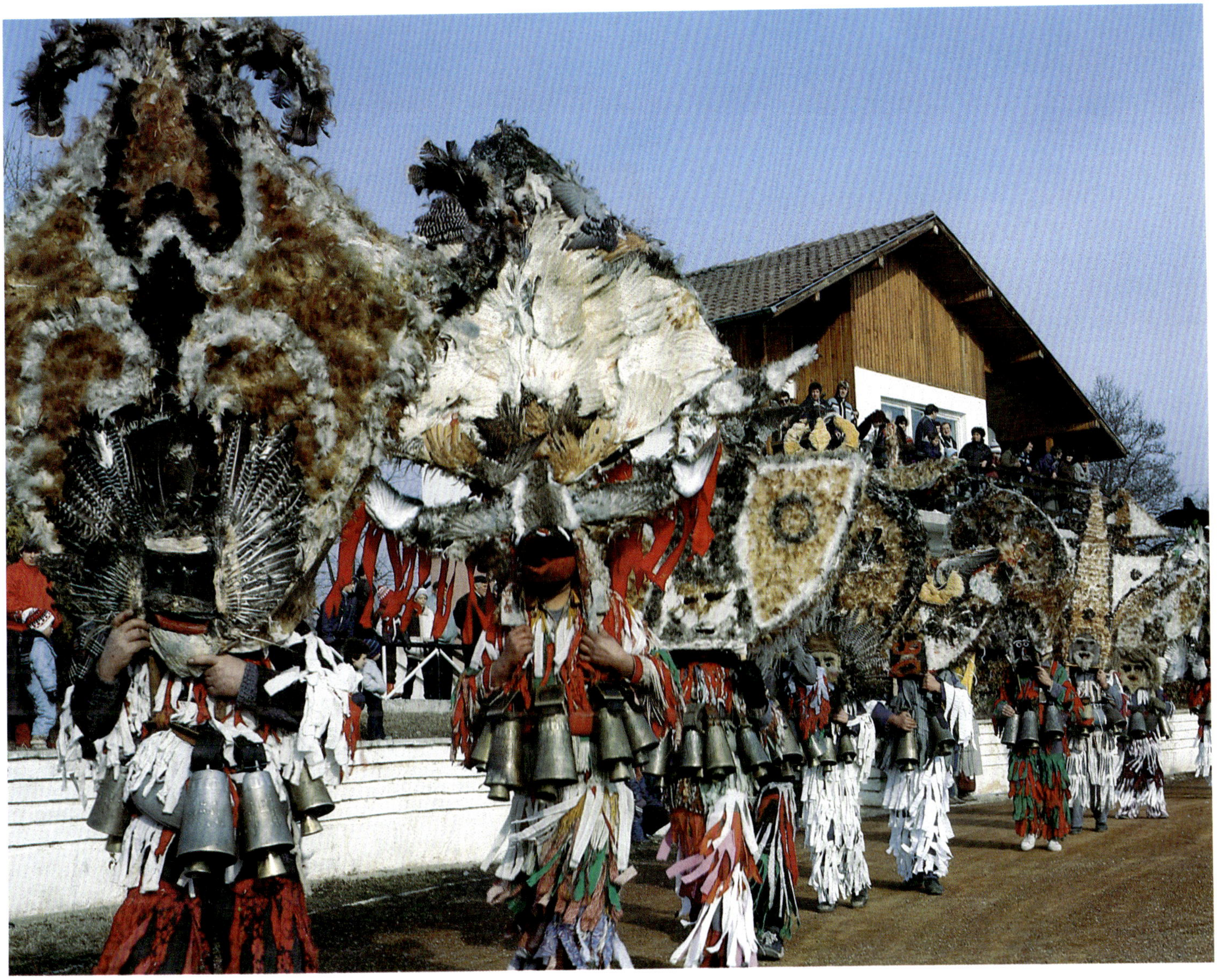

Growers, and St. George's Day, as the Day of Shepherds. Even in official civic ceremonies, such as weddings, giving a name to a newborn baby and other occasions, traditional symbols are used: such as ritual loaves of bread, flowers and pouring of water.
Endless examples can be cited and they will reveal the variety of forms through which the most valuable, the most promising and intransient elements in the traditional culture of the Bulgarian people is penetrating the daily and festive life of modern generations.
The dialectics of the traditional cultural heritage in the present-day ethnic and cultural process of the Bulgarian nation, is one of the most important mechanisms responsible for the identity and originality of Bulgarian culture today.
In this sense the parallels that can be drawn between the traditional cultural heritage in Great Britain and in Bulgaria, would reveal once again the enormous variety of paths followed by the world cultural processes and the contribution of each country to its enrichment and diversification.

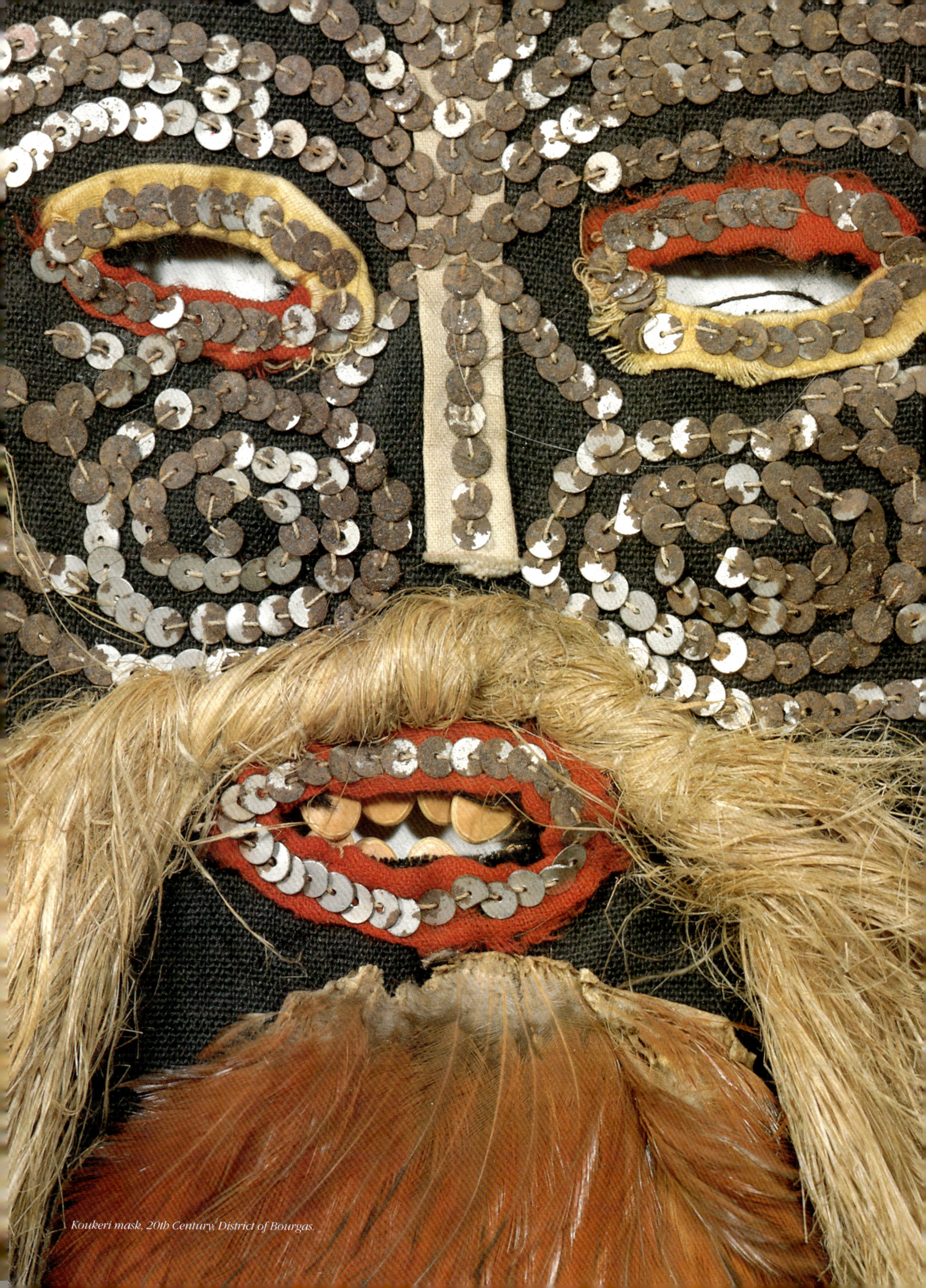

Koukeri mask, 20th Century, District of Bourgas.

Holidays and Customs

Roumyana Danova

Holidays and customs are an inseparable part of the culture of the traditional Bulgarian society. They carry a rich symbolism and accompany the life of every Bulgarian who becomes the carrier and the perpetrator of folk traditions. Holidays and customs reflect the specificity of many archaic rituals inherited from the ancient Thracians, Slavs and Proto-Bulgarians.

The various props and paraphenalia for the rituals occupy a place of prominence in the customs and holidays, with their bright originality and symbolism. The decorated cornel twigs (*sourvaknitsa*), the twisted tasselled red and white thread symbolising spring and health (*martenitsa*), the masks of the *koukeri* (mummers), the ritual costumes, the articles of adornment and the nosegays, and especially the moulded decoration on the ritual loaves of bread, are a materialisation of the feelings, ideas and dreams of the folk artist. Being organically linked to the customs, the ritual paraphenalia and props are a singular messenger of the ancient culture of our ancestors.

Ritual practice in the customs, although active until the end of the 19th century, gradually began to fade away and to lose its initial meaning. The symbolism of the ritual paraphenalia began to be reinterpreted. By altering the functions, it came to be perceived more and more as a work having some ethnic characteristics, an example of folk art. This was best illustrated in the *martenitsas, sourvaknitsas*, the painted Easter eggs, the masks and ritual loaves of bread.

The traditional holidays are of a labour, calendar and family character and they are closely interconnected. The first type comprises the rituals and customs connected with rain and drought. Calendar holidays are provisionally divided into winter, spring and summer festivities, though without a very sharp differentiation because many rites are mutually complementary or are performed several times a year in different customs.

The winter holidays start at the end of the calendar year, i.e. from Ignazhden (December 19th), and comprise Christmas, the New Year, St. Basil's Day (*Sourvaki*) and *Babin Den* (the day of midwives). In the beginning of the year celebrations focus around the following holidays: Epiphany (January 6th), St. John's Day (January 7th), *Trifon Zarezan* (St. Tryphon's Day - February 14th), *Koukerov Den* on Cheese Shrovetide and *Todorovden* (St. Theodore's Day).

The spring holidays start with the welcoming of *Baba Marta* on March 1st and follow with the Day of the Annuciation (March 25th), St. Lazarus' Day and Easter. St. George's Day (May 6th) is the biggest traditional holiday between spring and summer and it is characterised by many agrarian elements. A holiday marking the end of spring is the Day of St. Constantine and St. Helena (May 21st), when fire games (fire dancing is typical of the Strandja region) are organised. It is interesting to note that the practice of fire-dancing is alive to this day.

The summer holidays start with Midsummer Day (June 24th), with special prominence being given to so-called dog-days around St. Marina's Day (July 17th). The beginning of the autumn holidays is considered to be marked by *Golyama Bogoroditsa* (The Day of the Dormition of the Mother of God-August 28th) while *Krustovden* (The Day ot the Elevation of the Cross) and *Dmitrovden* (the Feast of St. Demetrius of Thessaloniki) are associated with the completion of the active annual agricultural cycle.

Rain bringing customs and rituals were also very widespread. They belonged to two main types: *peperuda* (*dodolo, pemperuga*) and *German*

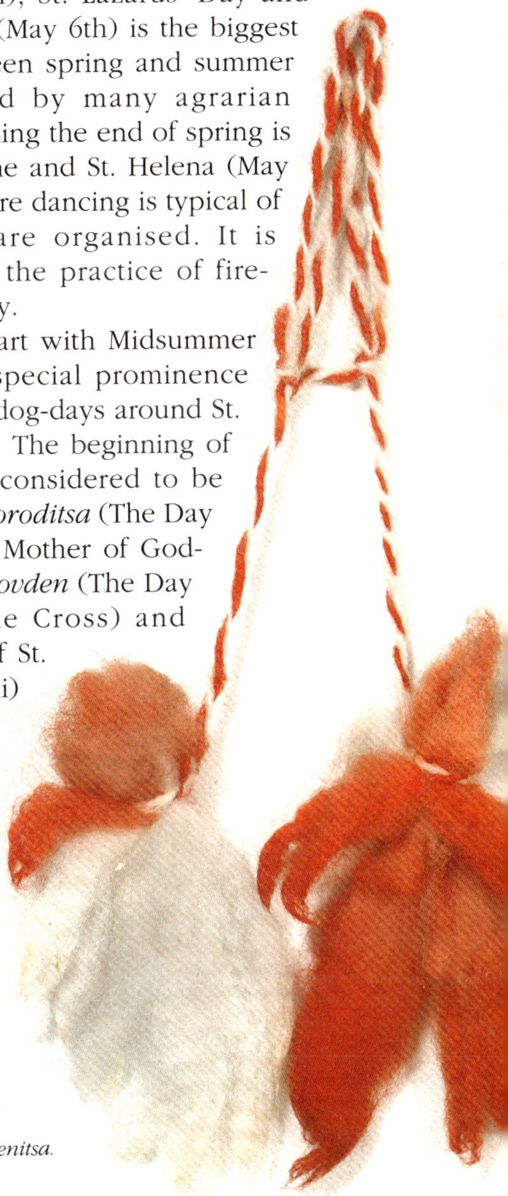

Martenitsa.

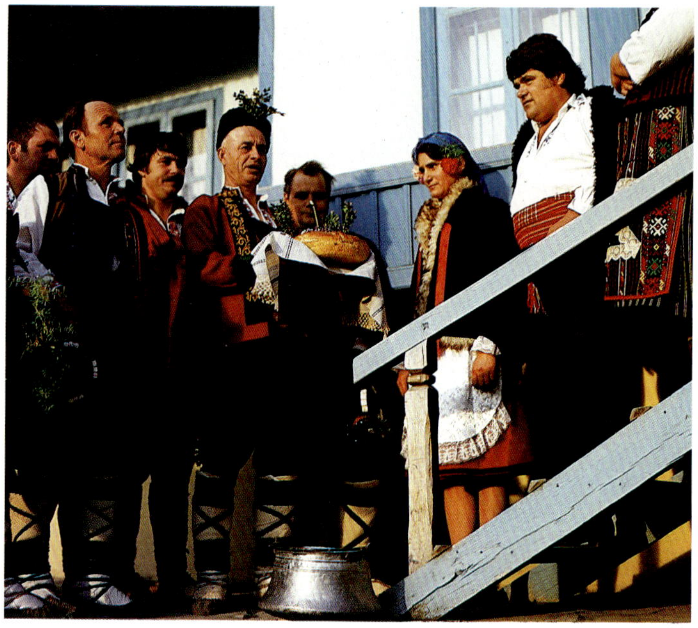

Sourvakar's blessing, District of Silistra.

(*Kabaivan, Kaloyan*) for invoking rain or drought. Labour customs were also very common, the most characteristic among them being the making of *brada* (*Bogova/Spasova brada*) at the end of the harvest. Building customs were also very popular.

The commemoration services and rituals for the dead occupy a prominent place in the traditional calendar as a manifestation of the cult of worshipping the ancestors. The commemorative customs are around Easter and Ascension Day in spring, around the Day of the Dormition of the Mother of God in summer and around the Day of the Archangel Michael in Autumn. The fires lit in connection with the commemoration practices are a particularly characteristic feature.

The most widespread among the family customs in the late 19th and early 20th century were the customs and practices connected with the baptising of the baby and with the wedding.

The Exhibition displays ritual objects related to some more important traditional holidays and customs from the winter and spring cycles, which are not sharply differentiated in principle. They illustrate characteristic rituals which make use of different ritual props and paraphenalia (both in their nature and in their symbolism) as well as blessings, songs and ritual clothes. An example can be found in the winter holidays from the late 19th and early 20th century, which comprise rites associated with bringing fertility to people and to the entire animal and plant world surrounding them. Some of their ritual practices have been preserved to this day. For example, one such ancient ritual that has survived to our times is the *koledouvane* (the Christmas carol-singing rounds). This is practiced in almost all regions of the country, being most widespread in the eastern part of Bulgaria, where many Christmas songs have been preserved, as well as blessings for health and fertility for every living creature in the home and outside it, "....may there be as much health in this house as there are many stars in the sky, Kolade...". The Christmas rounds are performed by young men who elect their leader, *stanenik* a respected and honoured man. He in his turn chooses a *blagoslovnik* who utters the blessings and the best wishes. The rounds start at the house of the *stanenik* as an expression of respect and then the other houses are visited. Very interesting is the ring-shaped bun made by the *stanenik*. It is decorated with sprigs of basil, strings of popcorn, maize and raisins as a symbol of fertility. Holding this ritual bun wrapped in a white towel in his hands, the *stanenik* makes the rounds, visiting each house and, through its symbols, brings to everyone health, affluence, fertility and joy, further reinforced by the Christmas carols and blessings. Another point of interest is offered by the various articles of adornment of the *koledari* nosegays of ivy and boxwood, strings of popcorn hanging around the fur hats of the *koledari* in Eastern Bulgaria and their wreaths made of dried prunes and lumps of sugar, trimmed with red thread, wound by young maidens (*podevki*) in Dobroudja. The decoration and the symbolism of the ritual loaves of bread and the ring-shaped buns is very rich and varied. They are prepared specially for Christmas and the buns are

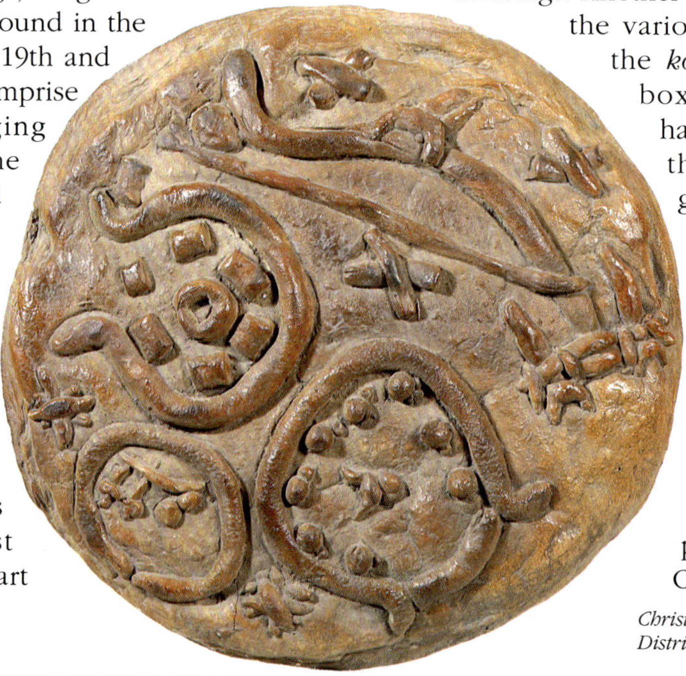

Christmas bread, 19th Century, District of Pernik.

given to the *koledari* who put them one over the other on their shepherd's crooks.

On *Sourvaki* (St. Basil's Day - January 1st) groups of young boys go from house to house. The boys (*sourvakari*) utter New Year's best wishes by tapping everyone on the back with their decorated cornel twigs (*sourvaknitsa*), which are an invariable element of this custom. The traditional rhyme with which health, fertility and well-being is wished goes like this;

Сурва, сурва година,
Весела година,
Голям клас на нива,
Червена ябълка в градина,
Жълт мамул на леса,
Голям грозд на лоза,
Пълна къща с деца,
Пълна кесия с пари.
Живо, здраво догодина,
Догодина, до амина!

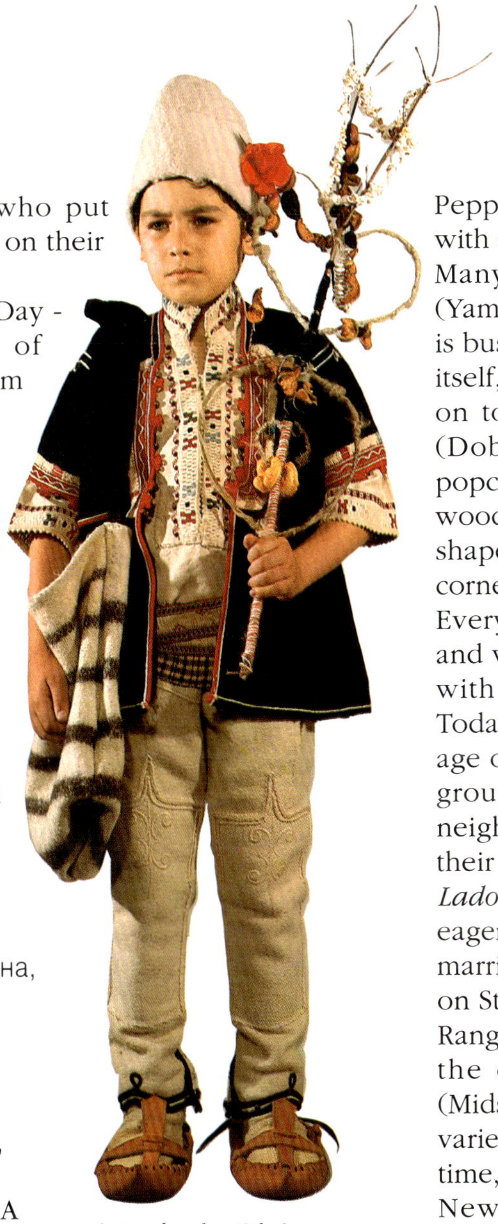

Sourvakarche, 19th Century, District of Sofia.

Beat, beat the year, A joyful year - Big ears of corn in the field, Red apples in the orchards, Yellow corn on the cobs, Large bunches of grape on the vines, A house full of children, A purse full of money, May we live happily until next year, Until next year - Amen.

The *sourvaknitsas* are very common all over the country. They are decorated by each of the *sourvakari* independently. They are made in two ways by cutting the bark of the cornel twig and by decorating its branches with wool, beans, popcorn, dried fruit, small bread rings, coins, etc. threaded on a red string. Peppers and garlic also appear as decorative elements with apotropaic power.

Many local variants exist. In Southeastern Bulgaria (Yambol district) the *sourvaknitsa* has many branches, is bushy, with notches and carved patterns in the wood itself, completed by a nosegay in the middle, an apple on top and ears of wheat. In Northeastern Bulgaria (Dobroudja) it is decorated with many strings of popcorn twisted around flower patterns cut from the wood itself. Balls of red wool, popcorn and small ring-shaped buns, dried fruit and garlic can be seen on the cornel twigs from Northern Bulgaria.

Every year the children decorate their *sourvaknitsas* and with the arrival of the New Year they tap everyone with them for health and well-being in the home. Today this ritual is performed by girls as well (up to the age of 12-13 years), but in the towns they do not go in groups from house to house, but tap the backs of neighbours, relatives and friends who have come to their house on the first day of the New Year.

Ladouvane is a custom that young girls look forward to eagerly because it is associated with fortune-telling for marriage by singing to rings. This custom is performed on St. Basil's Day in Western Bulgaria, along the Balkan Range and partly along the Danube river. In the rest of the country the rite is performed on *Enyovden* (Midsummer Day), when it is called *Enyova boulya.* A variety of this custom is the rite performed at harvest-time, when it is called "the singing of the swaphooks".

New Year's customs with masked performers are widespread predominantly in Western Bulgaria. They are performed on *"Sourva"* and therefore the participants are called *sourvakari, vassilichari,* or *eshkari.* Their most essential feature is the ritual masks resembling animals such as bears, foxes, wolves, birds and other fantastic animals. Similar New Year's customs exist among the other Slav nations as well, betraying many common features both in the costumes and in the masks, which suggests a common Slav origin.

Trifon Zarezan is celebrated in the vine-growing regions on St. Tryphon's Day (February 14th) when the vines are cut. The rites on this day are on an agrarian

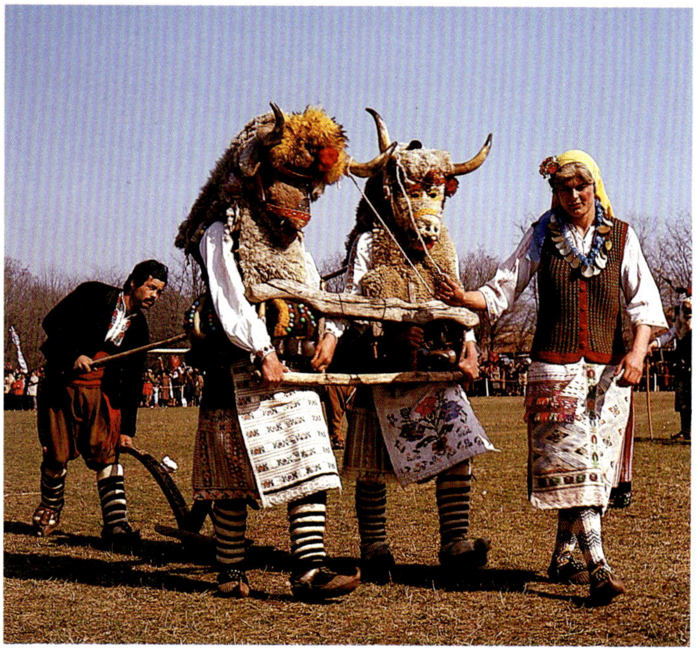

Ritual ploughing by Koukeri, District of Yambol.

basis and they are connected with the rejuvenation of nature, which refers the custom to the spring rites. *Todorovden* (St. Theodore's Day) is also close to the spring rites and customs, because it is celebrated to give health and strength to horses. The rite comprises agricultural ritual elements, as well as elements with a solar connotation, which are incidentally part of many other rites connected with the use of ritual fire.

Koukov/Koukerov den (the day of the *koukeri*) is similar to the games of the *sourvakari*. It is celebrated most often on Cheese Shrovetide (the first Sunday before Lent), i.e. on the verge between winter and spring and in the beginning of the new agricultural year. The customs has deep roots that can be traced to Thracian antiquity. In addition to being connected with a concrete community, it also has a clear agrarian orientation. The persons taking part in the ritual and the ritual practices (ploughing-in, planting of the seed), should guarantee fertility through imitative magic actions.

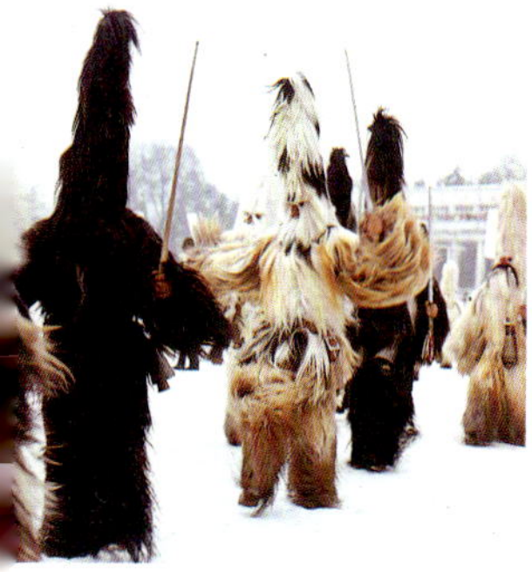

Babougeri procession, District of Blagoevgrad.

The *koukeri* are men dressed in carnival costumes and wearing belts on which bells of different sizes are hanging. On their heads they have masks of various wild and domestic animals. The *koukeri* move around in large groups, jumping and making an incredible noise in order to chase away the old year and the evil forces. The higher the *koukeri* jump, the taller will be the wheat in that year.

These customs, which are still alive and active, have now acquired the form of village carnivals that have preserved the entire ancient symbolism. They contribute to bringing closer together the people from the respective communities and symbolize the arrival of the beautiful spring days. The whole ceremony is fraught with emotion and excitement for participants and spectators alike. No less emotion has gone into the preparing of the masks and the costumes. Every participant in the ritual makes his own mask and costume with a lot of imagination and zeal. Recently there seems to be something of a competition for the best mask, costume and ritual group among individual participants, groups and even entire villages or towns. The ancient semantic content is being replaced by the awareness that these practices help keep alive the ethnic tradition, at the same time promoting the functions of the games as show and entertainment.

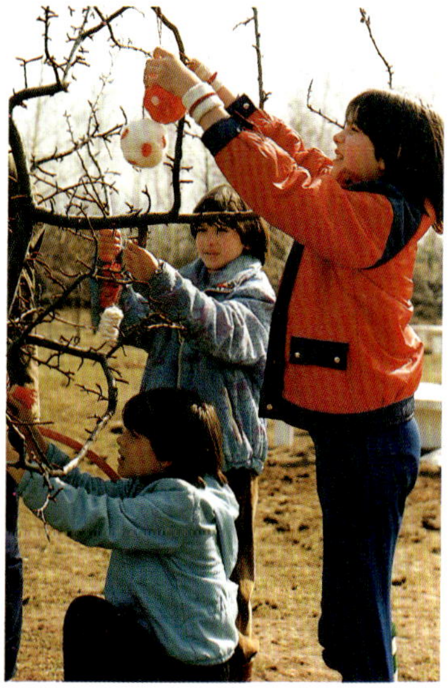

The first day of Spring – hanging Martenitsi on a tree.

In folk beliefs Spring starts in March therefore all festivities during this month are joyful and vital. They reflect the anticipation of the awakening of Nature from its winter sleep, they are connected with the day of the Spring equinox and the beginning of the new agrarian and stock-breeding year.

Particularly interesting are the rites performed on March 1st before sunrise (cleaning and sweeping), which represent a symbolic chasing away of winter, strengthened by the purifying power of the fires that are being lit. It is a very common practice to jump over the fire "like a cross for health" and also as a magic sign for protection. The practice of taking out red textiles and red clothes in front of the house or under the eaves of the roof on March 1st possesses a very pronounced protective and productive function. A similar function is also detected in the wearing of

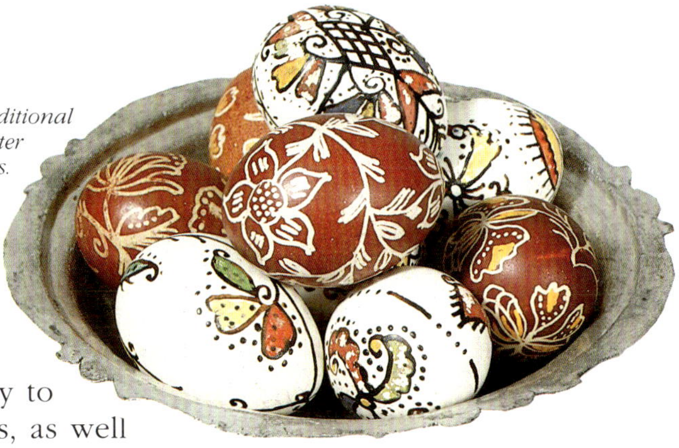

Traditional Easter eggs.

martenitsas, which is one of the most essential and widespread rituals on March 1st.

The *martenitsa* is a specific ritual attribute. It is usually made of white and red wood (or twisted threads), with other colours being added in some regions. *Martenitsas* were tied on March 1st on people and domestic animals, on fruit-bearing trees and on objects like distaffs, weaving-looms and spinning-wheels, as well as on some farm buildings. The principal material is usually wool, but other materials were added because they were believed to have apotropaic power; garlic, a blue bead, a coin, etc., which emphasises the character of the *martenitsa* as a kind of amulet. Today the only surviving custom connected with the first day of March is the ubiquitous practice of tying *martenitsas* and giving them to people with best wishes for health and longevity.

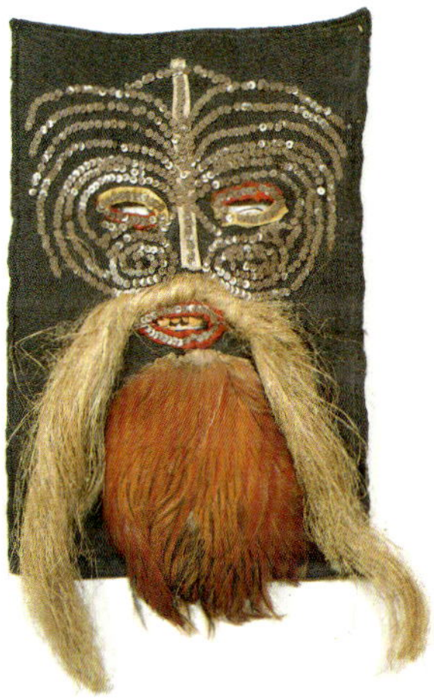

Koukeri mask, 20th Century, District of Bourgas.

Other ancient customs and holidays between Spring and Autumn are associated with the most important Christian holidays of the Bulgarians - Easter and St. George's Day. The painted Easter eggs with their fruit bearing and productive semanticism are made in every home for this day. In the regions of Ihtiman, Pazardjik, Etropole, Samokov, Velingrad and elsewhere there is still a living tradition of painting the eggs in two or three colours, using wax to produce characteristic floral, geometric and more rarely zoomorphic elements as well.

Gergyovden (St. George's Day) with its many surviving agrarian elements is best preserved among stockbreeding and especially shepherding communities in the country. The rituals and customs related to this day reflect elements of blood and bloodletting sacrifice, the magic function of various rites for bringing health and fertility to the animals, as well as elements of the solar semantic circle. *Gergyovden* is celebrated today as the day of the shepherd and stockbreeders and ritual practices have been preserved, albeit stripped of their original meaning.

Among the family holidays the wedding has remained an active and joyous occasion, preserving the rich rituals associated with this event. Some ritual practices connected with the arrangement of the wedding between the families of the bride and bridegroom, the entering of the newlyweds into their new home, the relations of the parents of the spouses and the ritual participants in the wedding, and the protectors of the young family have still survived. Rites aimed at guaranteeing health, prosperity and fertility in the family occur in this group of traditional holidays, as well as rites with a purifying and apotropaic orientation.

The splendid ritual props and paraphernalia, together with ritual customs, enrich the holiday. Ritual loaves of bread are made for the principal participants in the ritual: the best man (*koum*) and his wife, the bride and bridegroom and the future in-laws, each of which is given a specific ornamentation. In many places there is still a practice of making a banner for the wedding, nosegays for the bridegroom's brothers and relatives and ritual vessels.

Many of the practices surviving from the remote past are resurrected again in the wedding ceremonies of today, including those held in the official ritual halls for weddings where the marriage is officially registered. In this way modern weddings are enriched with beautiful and deeply symbolic elements.

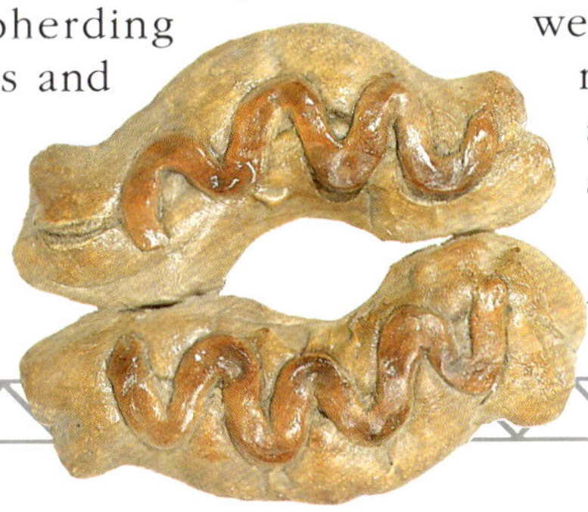

Bread for St. George's Day, 19th Century, District of Elhovo.

Map of Bulgaria

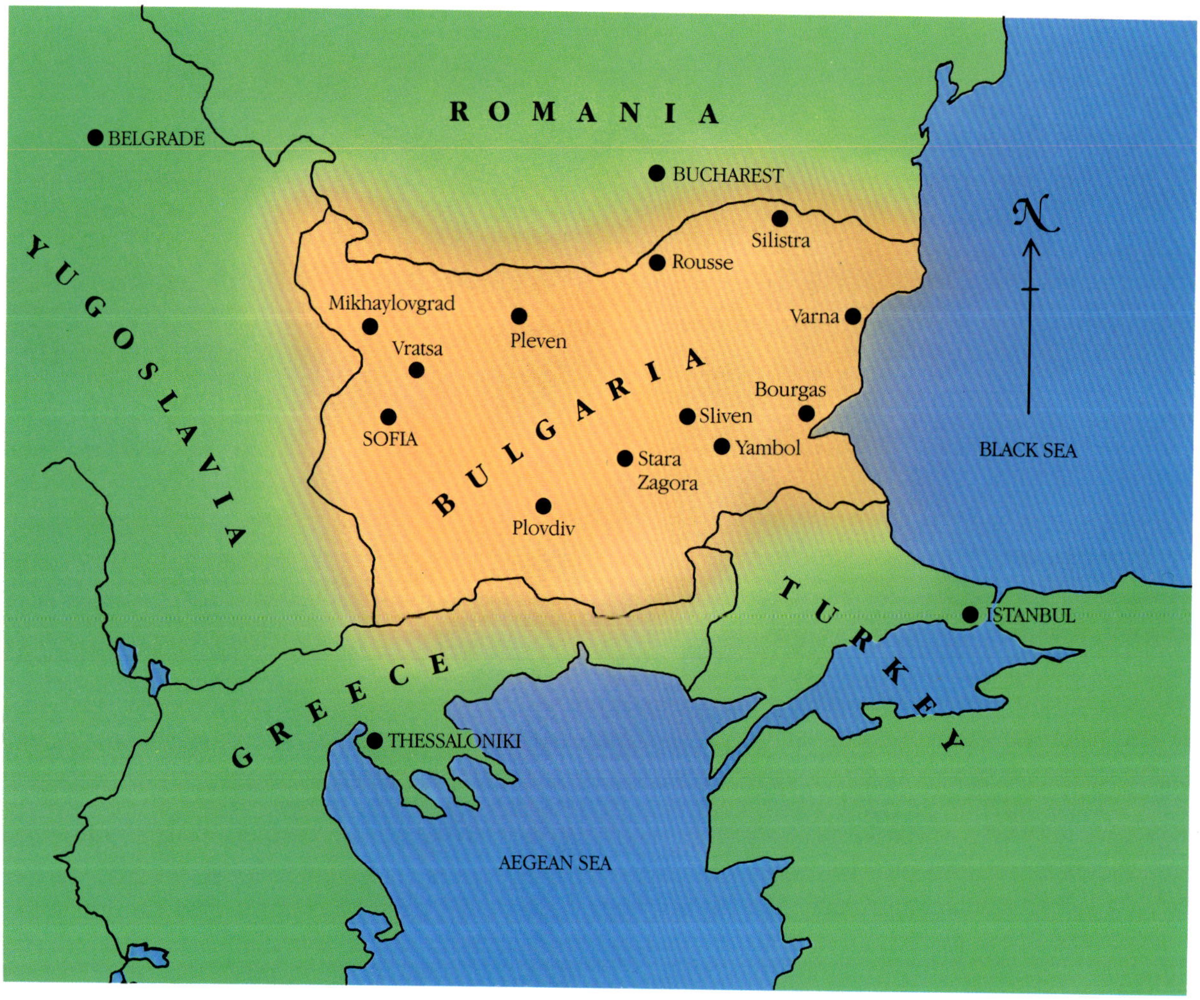

Bibliography

PUBLICATIONS IN ENGLISH

NICOLOFF, Assen. *Bulgarian Folklore, Cleveland, 1975.*

NICOLOFF, Assen. *Bulgarian Folktales, Cleveland, 1975.*

BOKOV, G. *Modern Bulgaria: History, Policy, Economy, Culture. Sofia, 1981.*

BOLL, Michael. *Cold War in the Balkans: American Foreign Policy and Emergence of Communist Bulgaria 1943-47. University Press of Kentucky, 1984.*

DUQUESNE UNIVERSITY. *The Folk Arts of Bulgaria – Papers presented at a Symposium, Pittsburgh, Pennsylvania, October 1976. Duquesne University Tamburitzans Institute of Folk Arts.*

GEORGIEVA, IVANICHKA. *Bulgarian Mythology, Svyat Publishers, Sofia, 1985.*

GROUEFF, Stephan. *Crown of Thorns; The Reign of King Boris III, 1918-1943 Madison Books, 1987.*

HASTIE, Roy Macgregor. *Modern Bulgarian Poetry, Sofia Press and University of Iowa, 1975.*

LAMPE, John R. *The Bulgarian Economy in the 20th Century Croom Helm, 1986.*

MACDERMOTT, Mercia. *The Apostle of Freedom: A portrait of Vassil Levsky. Sofia Press, Sofia, 1979.*

MOSER, Charles. *A History of Modern Bulgarian Literature 1865-1944. Mouton, Paris, 1972.*

RADEV, Stoyan. *Anglo-Bulgarian Relations since the 2nd World War, Sofia Press, 1981.*

SHANNON, Richard. *Gladstone and the Bulgarian Agitation 1876. Harvester Press/Archon Books, London, 1975.*

TODOROV, Nikolai. *A Short History of Bulgaria, Sofia Press, Sofia, 1975.*

VENEDIKOV & BOYADJIEV. *Bulgaria's Treasures from the Past F.L.P., Sofia, 1965.*

BULGARIA: *Past and Present (2 vols), Sofia, 1982.*

PUBLICATIONS IN BULGARIAN

Periodicals:

MISCELLANY FOR FOLK WISDOM, SCIENCE AND LITERATURE. *I – XLIII: 1889, 1942, XLIV: 1949-1985, continuing.*

BULGARIAN ETHNOGRAPHY. *1-4 Issue 1 published 1975, continuing 4 books yearly. From 1990, 6 books yearly.*

BULGARIAN FOLKLORE. *1-4. Issue 1 published 1975, continuing, 4 books yearly.*

BULLETIN OF THE INSTITUTE AND MUSEUM OF ETHNOGRAPHY, *b-14: 1953-1975.*
Bulletin of the National Ethnographic Museum. 1923-1943.

COLLECTIVE MONOGRAPHS AND COLLECTIONS:

BULGARIAN FOLK CULTURE. *(Historical and Ethnographical article), Sofia, 1981.*

BULGARIAN FOLK ART. *Sofia, 1979.*

ETHNOGRAPHY OF BULGARIA. *Vol. 1. 1980; Vol. II, 1983; Vol. III, 1985.*

POPULAR CUSTOMS AND CULTURES OF THE OLD BULGARIAN POPULATION IN NORTH-EAST BULGARIA. *Sofia, 1985.*

TRADITION IN CONTEMPORARY FOLK-FESTIVE AND RITUAL SYSTEM. *Sofia, 1983.*

AUTHOR'S WORKS:

ARBALIEV, G. *National Traditions in Architecture, Sofia, 1982.*

BLAGOEVA, S. *Bulgarian Folk Adornments, Sofia, 1977.*

DRUMEV, D. & VASILEV, A. *The Wood-carving Art in Bulgaria Sofia, 1955.*

GENCHEV, S. *Folk Culture and Ethnography, Sofia, 1984.*

GENCHEV, S. *The Wedding, Bulgarian Holidays and Customs, Sofia, 1987.*

GEORGIEV, G. *The Liberation and the Ethnocultural Evolution of the Bulgarian People 1878-1900, Sofia, 1979.*

GEORGIEVA, I. *Bulgarian Folk Mythology, Sofia, 1983.*

KRUSTEVA-NOJAROVA, G. *Traditional Home Weaving and Ornamental Textiles in Bulgaria, Sofia, 1981.*

MIKOV, L. *Easter Eggs in Bulgaria. Bulgarian Holidays and Customs, Sofia, 1982.*

STANKOV, D. *Rugs and Carpets, Sofia, 1975.*

VELEVA, M. & VENEDIKOVA, V. *Textiles and Textile Techniques in South-east and North-west Bulgaria, Sofia, 1967.*

ZLATEV, I. *The Bulgarian House During the Renaissance, Sofia, 1955.*